EXPERIENCING *the* GREAT I AM

40 Faith-Building Stories from Contemporary Christians

BRYANT & CINDY HEFLIN

EDITORS

Kregel
Publications

Experiencing the Great I Am: 40 Faith-Building Stories from Contemporary Christians

© 2005 by Bryant and Cindy Heflin

Published by Kregel Publications, a division of Kregel, Inc., P.O. Box 2607, Grand Rapids, MI 49501.

Library of Congress Cataloging-in-Publication Data
Heflin, Bryant.
Experiencing the great I am: 40 faith-building stories from contemporary Christians / by Bryant & Cindy Heflin.
    p. cm.
Included bibliographical references.
    1. Devotional calendars. I. Heflin, Cindy. II. Title.
BV4810.H45   2005
242—dc22   2005006555

ISBN 0-8254-2779-7

Printed in the United States of America

05 06 07 08 09 / 5 4 3 2 1

With love

to

Krista and Jessica.

When life's journey brings you to the mountaintop and through the darkest valley, fix your gaze on Jesus. The One who neither slumbers nor sleeps will watch over you and lead you on to abundant life!

Jesus said,

"The thief comes only to steal, and kill, and destroy; I came that they may have life, and might have it abundantly" (John 10:10 NASB).

And

with humble adoration to our heavenly Father:

"Be exalted, O God, above the heavens; let your glory be over all the earth" (Psalm 57:11).

Contents

Acknowledgments

Words alone cannot express the depth of gratitude in our hearts for our heavenly Father, who has enabled this endeavor to become a reality. We are humbled and honored to be part of this awesome adventure. Thank You, Jesus, for faithfully leading and guiding every step of the way. To You alone be all the glory!

We are grateful to God for all who contributed to this project and extend our heartfelt appreciation to—

Our daughters, Krista and Jessica: You girls are the best! Your love, prayers, patience, and sacrifice beyond measure enabled us to remain faithful to this God-given task. We are proud of you and your commitment to live for Christ. Our greatest joy is to see you walk in His truth.

Cindy's parents, Don and Carole Puls: You have always been a steadfast source of unfailing love, strength, and encouragement to us. We express our sincere love and gratitude to you both. Thank you for imparting the gift of compassion and perseverance through your lifelong example.

Bryant's parents, Malen and Zelma Heflin: You are dearly missed. We remember you for your devotion to your family and your faithfulness to God. Thank you for always being an example of spiritual strength in the face of adversity. Although your health often failed, your faith never faltered.

Our family and friends: Each of you has greatly enriched our lives. Thank you for your love, support, encouragement, and especially your prayers.

Marita Littauer and the CLASServices staff: Special thanks for your commitment to encourage, inspire, and instruct—with excellence.

Wayne Holmes: Our heartfelt thanks for your genuine friendship, and for generously sharing your expertise, experience, and encouragement.

Beth Moore: Thank you for teaching us to apply the important biblical principles of *Praying God's Word* and *Believing God*—for the impossible.

The many writers who submitted their stories: We were touched by every testimony received, and wish that each one could have been included.

Our awesome team of readers: Special thanks for the many hours you spent reading and reviewing submissions, and for the valuable input you provided.

Don Puls, Sharon Jergens, Sue Cutting, Krista Heflin, and Jessica Heflin: God bless you for your excellent assistance and manuscript review. Your generosity helped to lighten our load.

Nancy Anderson: Heartfelt thanks and hugs for your friendship, encouragement, and expert editorial assistance.

Lois Pecce: Our sincere gratitude for the countless hours, valuable input, and editorial expertise you have generously given on behalf of this project. You are truly heaven-sent—a mentor and a friend.

Our contributing authors: Thank you for sharing your stories and your faith. May your testimonies encourage and minister to others as they have encouraged and ministered to us.

The first-class team at Kregel Publications: We are grateful for your expertise and commitment to excellence. Thank you for believing in this project and granting us the opportunity to encourage others to experience the Great I Am!

Introduction

Do you desire to experience a closer walk with God; to know the depths of His love, the joy of His presence, and the richness of His mercy and grace—as you've never known before? Do you long to experience a deeper faith and live the abundant life in Christ each day?

God created us for this very purpose.

But sometimes . . . life throws us a curve. Disappointments mount. Despair sets in. With our eyes fixed on our sorrows, we hardly feel joy in God's presence. Can we truly stand firm in our faith and walk in victory when the storms of life roll in?

Nudged from my peaceful slumber by the radio alarm, I fumbled for the snooze bar. The announcer's voice filtered into my mind and seized my attention.

"While battling cancer, Barbara," the radio host addressed his guest, "you endured two unsuccessful surgeries, and then a third in which you suffered a punctured lung. As a Christian, how did you handle these devastating circumstances?"

"At times it was quite difficult," Barbara admitted. "Then, while forced by the lung injury to lie immobile for an entire week, I discovered this life-changing truth: By God's grace, I absolutely have the power to choose joy and trust God unconditionally!"

My eyes flashed open as this potent truth struck my heart. The strength of Barbara's faith was refreshing—and rare. Instantly, I recalled a conversation from the day before.

My friend Lisa sat at my kitchen table with a cappuccino in her hand and a faraway look in her eyes. Her somber expression revealed the pain of her broken heart.

I listened compassionately as Lisa spilled her anguish. A chronic illness, a rebellious teenage son, a marriage shattered beyond repair.

"My life is hopeless," she sighed. "Why has God abandoned me?" Staring into her cup, she continued, "I pray, but how can I trust God when nothing ever changes?"

As we talk with believers like Barbara and Lisa, and as we face times of trial in our own lives, one thing is clear: adversity has the potential to strengthen our faith—or destroy it.

Unfortunately, many in the body of Christ have fallen victim to what Jim Cymbala calls "'the Big-D'—discouragement." He observes that discouragement's "dreadful toll on the people of God is greater than anyone can calculate."[1] Sadly, many of us turn away from God just when we need Him most.

Why is standing firm in our faith so challenging? Can we truly experience the victorious life in Christ as God intended?

"In this world you will have trouble," Jesus said. "But take heart! I have overcome the world" (John 16:33b).

Adversity is inevitable. Pain, trouble, and heartache strike all who travel the road of life—the Bible guarantees it. Daily demands and disappointments unravel our spiritual stamina. Despair abounds. When life spirals out of control, countless battle-weary Christians falter in their faith and are dragged into defeat. In the heat of crisis, some of us even give up on God.

Adversity is inevitable, but it's also an invitation. Our heavenly Father beckons us to be still and know Him, to experience His love anew, to lift our downcast eyes and behold a glimpse of His glory so brilliant that earthly cares fade from sight! A man named Moses, worn and weary from shouldering the responsibilities of leadership, accepted this invitation to experience God. So, high atop Mount Sinai, the Great I Am "passed in front of Moses and said, 'I am the LORD, I am the LORD, the merciful and gracious God. I am slow to anger and rich in unfailing love and faithfulness.' ... Moses immediately fell to the ground and worshiped" (Exodus 34:6, 8 NLT).

Like Moses, when we encounter the living God it will change us forever! Experiencing a revelation of His divine nature and attributes enables us to know Him as He longs to be known. Then, as we focus on who He is—not on our struggles—we develop a "spiritual tunnel vision" that empowers us to overcome discouragement and spiritual defeat. This divine perspective leads us to the abundant life that God intends all believers to enjoy in His presence forever.

Adversity is inevitable, but trusting God is a choice. As we travel the path set before us, we will never face life's challenges alone if we depend on Jesus to guide us through every valley victoriously. The joy of the Christian life is not reserved for the mountaintop; it's found in knowing, trusting, and resting in Jesus Christ every step of the way.

Experiencing the Great I Am is a unique collection of forty personal testimonies; powerful examples of faith-filled believers overcoming adversity to the glory of God! These men, women, and teens encounter pain, doubt, fear, and defeat along their spiritual journey. Yet, with a bold step of faith, each marvels to discover what the Father was longing to reveal—a facet of His character that they had never known! Despite their struggles, each believer's faith is strengthened, and their hope restored as they focus on the Father and experience specific attributes of His divine identity in new and life-changing ways. A closer walk with Jesus fills them with joy, peace, and the strength to stand firm in the midst of the storm.

Each dynamic account and Bible promise included in *Experiencing the Great I Am* can help you to:

- Experience a specific attribute of God's divine nature
- Restore hope and strengthen faith
- Discover the remedy for spiritual discouragement
- Recognize Jesus Christ as your true source of hope in times of trial

Our desire is for this book to be like time spent with a treasured friend. May it provide you with the hope and spiritual encouragement you need. We pray that these powerful accounts will not only calm your anxious heart and bolster your fragile faith, but also kindle—even ignite—a passion in your life for a deeper relationship with God.

Our prayer is that all who read these encouraging testimonies will lift their eyes to the One who holds the victory in their own circumstances—and experience the Great I Am!

Our light and momentary troubles are achieving for us an eternal glory that far outweighs them all. So we fix our eyes not on what is seen, but on what is unseen. For what is seen is temporary, but what is unseen is eternal.

—2 Corinthians 4:17–18

PART 1

EXPERIENCE HIS FAITHFULNESS

We Can Trust Him to Keep His Promises

The Greatest Lesson

JENNIFER ROTHSCHILD

And the peace of God, which transcends all understanding,
will guard your hearts and your minds in Christ Jesus.

—PHILIPPIANS 4:7

Life is a fascinating school. Tucked in the corners of its dailiness are countless lessons, large and small. Some I've learned as a matter of course, almost unconsciously. Others have frustrated all of my attempts to comprehend. I've raised my hand time and again in life's classroom, longing for answers. I've scrutinized the pages of its textbook, yearning to understand. I've walked its hallways and climbed its stairs, searching for its meaning.

We learn many of life's lessons when times are good and circumstances are easy. Others we learn only in seasons of hardship, loss, and great darkness. Although suffering can be the harshest of headmasters, its curriculum may open the door to freedom beyond our loftiest expectations. Sometimes it's only in the adversity we dread that we begin to discover the kind of life we've only dreamed of.

That was the lesson God began to teach me in 1979.

I began my sophomore year of high school experiencing all of the usual teenage changes. But there had also been one very unusual one. Near the end of junior high school, I began to realize that my eyesight was deteriorating.

As I picked my way carefully through the packed hallways of Glades Junior High, I was amazed at how my classmates streamed through the crowd with such ease—even in dark stairwells. How could they do that without bumping into schoolmates or lockers? When we played softball in P.E., I couldn't understand how my teammates could catch the ball so easily. I would stand out in right field, glove in hand, and stare intently at the ground, trying to see the shadow of the approaching ball. Then I'd listen to where it landed and hope I could find it.

My math grades were beginning to drop because, even though I didn't know it at the time, I couldn't see the difference between a 3 and an 8. My friends could see the numbers on the telephone pad whereas I hadn't been able to see the numbers on my locker for months.

As difficult as it was to admit, I began to realize that it wasn't normal for me not to be able to see a softball in the air, the stairs in a stairwell, or the numbers written on a blackboard. As a result, I began to feel more awkward and self-conscious. At last, I became so concerned that I told my mother, who (as you might imagine) immediately took me to an ophthalmologist.

The eye doctor tried to remedy my failing sight with prescriptions for stronger glasses, but they didn't help. Eventually, he referred me to an eye hospital.

After several days of testing, the doctors at the Bascom Palmer Eye Institute met with my folks and me in a conference room. They told us that I had retinitis pigmentosa, a degenerative disease that slowly eats away the retina of the eye.

There was no cure, and no way to correct the damage already done.

The doctors said I had lost so much vision that, at fifteen, I was already legally blind. And they told us that my retinas would continue to deteriorate until I was totally blind.

Blind . . . totally blind.

The words sounded so final. So certain. So cold. I felt a chill inside that I'd never felt. Maybe that's what finality feels like. It was almost surreal.

Nothing else was said. Silence fell upon that conference room like shadows fall just before night, and it shrouded us as we left the hospital, walked across the parking lot, got into the car, and journeyed home. I have often thought that it was probably much harder for my parents that day than it was for me. Yes, my eyes were being robbed of sight, but their hearts were being crushed. Can you imagine their heartache? Can you hear the sound of that door slamming in their souls? Surely one of life's greatest sorrows must be to watch your child suffer—and to feel helpless to prevent it.

My dad gripped the steering wheel tightly as he piloted us home through the spidery Miami streets. I could only imagine the prayers he must have been praying. He had always been my source of wisdom, my counselor, my comforter, my rescuer, and the one man I trusted completely. And even though he had also been my pastor, not even more than twenty years of ministry could have prepared him for this moment. I wonder if he was thinking, *Dear Lord, how can I fix this?*

Yet on the ride home he was silent.

My mother sat next to him in the front seat. I could feel her broken heart. A mother's heart is so tender. I don't know any mother who wouldn't willingly trade her own comfort to ease the suffering of her child. I wonder what her prayers were like on that day. My mom was my standard, my cheerleader, my encourager, my mentor, and my friend. I think she must have been wondering, *Will she be safe?*

Yet on the ride home she, too, was silent.

I had always been strong-willed, trusting, sensitive, and talkative. Yet, sitting in the back seat on the ride home that day, I also kept silent. I remember the reasons for my silence as if it were yesterday. My heart was swelling with emotion, and my mind was racing with questions and thoughts. *How will I finish high school? Will I ever go away to college? How will I know what I look like? Will I ever get a date or a boyfriend? Will I ever get married?* I remember feeling my fingertips and wondering how in the world people read Braille.

And then it hit me.

I would never be able to drive a car.

Like most teenagers, I thought that having wheels was just like having wings. I couldn't wait to drive! That was a step toward independence to which nothing else compared. But now it was a rite of passage I would never experience, and I was crushed.

After forty-five long minutes, we arrived home. Once inside, I went immediately to the living room and sat down at our piano. It was old and stately and had a warm, comforting sound. For me it was a place of refuge.

By then, I had been playing the piano for several years. In fact, I'd had almost five years of lessons. The funny thing about my lessons, though, was that I'd managed to stretch them out over an eight-year period. I was one of those kids who would *beg* my mother to let me take piano lessons—and then after about six months *beg* her to let me quit! Three or four months later, we'd start the whole routine over again.

I barely muddled through my lessons with many piano teachers, and I'm sure it wasn't pleasant for the listener to hear me practice what I'd learned. Let's just say that I was a little short on natural talent! I did, however, practice diligently every night after dinner. That's because if I did, I was excused from clearing the table and washing the dishes.

But this time was different.

I wasn't seeking refuge from chores, and I didn't play just the few songs I'd memorized. Instead, I began to play by ear, and the melody that filled the living room that afternoon belonged to a song I'd never played before. My fingers followed a pattern along the keyboard that was new to me, yet . . . somehow familiar. The song I played was "It Is Well with My Soul."

I think God guided my heart and hands to play that hymn. Some people have told me it was a miracle that I could sit down at the piano that day and begin to play by ear for the first time. Perhaps it was. Who knows? But to me, there was a bigger miracle that day, that dark day of shock, loss, and quiet sorrow.

The real miracle was not that I played "It Is Well with My Soul" but that it actually *was* well with my soul.

On that day more than twenty years ago—in the hospital, on the ride home, and at the piano—even as I mourned my loss, I looked into the heart of my Teacher. I knew His Word and His character, and they were what allowed me to say, "Whatever my lot . . . it is well with my soul."

Today I still sit at the piano and play by ear. I listen to books on tape. I walk with a cane and rely on others to drive me places. I know well the trappings of blindness. I understand the isolation and hardships it can bring. Yes, blindness can be painful—all life's heartaches are—but through it, God has taught me the greatest lesson to be learned in the school of suffering: *Even when it is not well with our circumstances, it can be well with our souls.*

That is the first and greatest lesson I learned in the dark, and the foundation for all of the lessons that have followed.

> When peace like a river attendeth my way,
> When sorrows like sea billows roll;
> Whatever my lot, Thou hast taught me to say,
> It is well, it is well with my soul.[1]

> Blessed are those who have learned to acclaim you,
>   who walk in the light of your presence, O LORD.
> They rejoice in your name all day long.
>   —Psalm 89:15–16

—————————————— *Prayer* ——————————————

Lord Jesus, in humble adoration I praise You for being my Prince of Peace! Thank You for Your faithfulness and Your promise to keep in perfect peace all who trust in You. May Your Spirit empower me to walk by faith, not by sight, through every uncertainty, distress, and affliction that comes my way. My heart shall rejoice in You forever. Amen.

A Personal Test

JIM CYMBALA

The righteous cry out, and the LORD hears them;
he delivers them from all their troubles.

—PSALM 34:17

All of my talking about prayer faced a severe test several years ago when Carol and I went through the darkest two-and-a-half-year tunnel we could imagine. Our oldest daughter, Chrissy, had been a model child growing up. But around age sixteen she started to stray. I admit that I was slow to notice it—I was too occupied with the church (The Brooklyn Tabernacle), starting branch congregations, overseeing projects, and all of the rest that ministry entails.

Meanwhile, Chrissy drew away from not only us but also God. In time, she even left our home. There were many nights when we had no idea where she was.

As the situation grew more serious, I tried everything. I begged, I pleaded, I scolded, I argued, I tried to control her with money. Looking back, I recognize the foolishness of my actions. Nothing worked; she just hardened more and more. Her boyfriend was everything we did not want for our child.

How I kept functioning through that period I don't know. Many a Sunday morning I would put on my suit, get into the car to drive to the tabernacle early, ahead of Carol, and cry for the next twenty-five minutes, all of the way to the church door. "God, how am I going to get through three meetings today? I don't want to make myself the center of attention. The people have problems of their own—they're coming for help and encouragement. But what about me? I'm hanging by a thread. Oh, God, please . . . my firstborn, my Chrissy."

Somehow God would pull my nerves together enough for me to function through another long Sunday. There were moments, however, as we were worshiping God and singing, that my spirit would almost seem to run away from the meeting to intercede for Chrissy. I had to control myself to stay focused on the people and their needs.

While this was going on, we learned that Carol needed an operation—a hysterectomy. As she tried to adjust afterward, the Devil took the opportunity to come after her and say, "You might have this big choir, and you're making albums and doing outreaches at Radio City Music Hall and all the rest. Fine. You and your husband can go ahead to reach the world for Christ—but I'm going to have your children. I've already got the first one. I'm coming for the next two."

Like any mother who loves her children, Carol was smitten with tremendous fear and distress. Her family meant more to her than a choir. One day she said to me, "Listen, we need to leave New York. I'm serious. This atmosphere has already swallowed up our daughter. We can't keep raising kids here. If you want to stay, you can—but I'm getting our other children out." She wasn't kidding.

I said, "Carol, we just can't do that. We can't *unilaterally* take off without knowing what God wants us to do."

Carol wasn't being rebellious; she was just depressed after the surgery. She elected not to pack up and run after all. And it was at that low point that she went to the piano one day, and God gave her a song that has touched more people than perhaps anything else she has written: *He's Been Faithful.*[1]

Were we calling on the Lord through all of this? In a sense we were. But I couldn't help jumping in to take action on my own, too. I was still, to some degree, the point guard wanting to grab the basketball, push it down the floor, make something happen, press through any hole in the defense I could find. But the more I pressed, the worse Chrissy got.

Then one November, I was alone in Florida when I received a call from a minister whom I had persuaded Chrissy to talk to. "Jim," he said, "I love you and your wife, but the truth of the matter is, Chrissy's going to do what Chrissy's going to do. You don't really have much choice, now that she's eighteen. She's determined. You're going to have to accept whatever she decides."

I hung up the phone. Something very deep within me began to cry out. "Never! I will never accept Chrissy's being away from you, Lord!" I knew that if she continued on the present path, there would be nothing but destruction awaiting her.

Once again, as back in 1972 when I became pastor of the floundering Brooklyn Tabernacle, there came a divine showdown. God strongly impressed me to stop crying, screaming, or talking to anyone else about Chrissy. I was to converse with no one but God. In fact, I knew that I should have no further contact with Chrissy—until God acted! I was just to believe and obey what I had preached so often: "Call upon Me in the day of trouble, and I will answer you." (See Psalm 50:15.)

I dissolved in a flood of tears. I knew I had to let go of this situation.

Back home in New York, I began to pray with an intensity and growing faith as never before. Whatever bad news I would receive about Chrissy, I kept interceding and actually began praising God for what I knew He would do soon. I made no attempts to see her. Carol and I endured the Christmas season with real sadness. I was pathetic, sitting around trying to open presents with our other two children—without Chrissy.

February came. One cold Tuesday night during the prayer meeting, I talked from Acts 4 about the church boldly calling on God in the face of persecution. We entered into a time of prayer, everyone reaching out to the Lord simultaneously.

An usher handed me a note. A young woman whom I felt to be spiritually sensitive had written, "Pastor Cymbala, I feel impressed that we should stop the meeting and all pray for your daughter."

I hesitated. Was it right to change the flow of the service and focus on my personal need?

Yet something in the note seemed to ring true. In a few minutes, I picked up a microphone and told the congregation what had just happened. "The truth of the matter," I said, "although I haven't talked much about it, is that my daughter is very far from God these days. She thinks up is down, and down is up; dark is light, and light is dark. But I know God can break through to her, and so I'm going to ask Pastor Boekstaaf to lead us in praying for Chrissy. Let's all join hands across the sanctuary."

As my associate began to lead the people, I stood behind him with my hand on his back. My tear ducts had run dry, but I prayed as best I knew.

To describe what happened in the next minutes, I can only employ a metaphor: The church turned into a labor room. The sounds of women giving birth are not pleasant, but the results are wonderful. Paul knew this when he wrote, "My dear children, for whom I am again in the pains of childbirth until Christ is formed in you . . ." (Gal. 4:19).

There arose a groaning, a sense of desperate determination, as if to say, "Satan, you will not have this girl. Take your hands off her—she's coming back!" I was overwhelmed. The force of that vast throng calling on God almost literally knocked me over.

When I got home that night, Carol was waiting up for me. We sat at the kitchen table drinking coffee, and I said, "It's over."

"What's over?" she wondered.

"It's over with Chrissy. You would have had to be in the prayer meeting tonight. I tell you, if there's a God in heaven, this whole nightmare is finally over." I described what had taken place.

Thirty-two hours later, on Thursday morning, as I was shaving, Carol suddenly burst through the door, her eyes wide. "Go downstairs!" she blurted. "Chrissy's here."

"*Chrissy's* here?"

"Yes! Go down!"

"But Carol—I—"

"Just go down," she urged. "It's you she wants to see."

I wiped off the shaving foam and headed down the stairs, my heart pounding. As I came around the corner, I saw my daughter on the kitchen floor, rocking on her hands and knees, sobbing. Cautiously I spoke her name, "*Chrissy?*"

She grabbed my pant leg and began pouring out her anguish. "Daddy—Daddy—I've sinned against God. I've sinned against myself. I've sinned against you and Mommy. Please forgive me. . . ."

My vision was as clouded by tears as hers. I pulled her up from the floor and held her close as we cried together.

Suddenly she drew back. "Daddy," she said with a start, "who was praying for me? Who was praying for me?" Her voice was like that of a cross-examining attorney.

"What do you mean, Chrissy?"

"On Tuesday night, Daddy—who was praying for me?" I didn't say anything, so she continued.

"In the middle of the night, God woke me and showed me I was heading toward this abyss. There was no bottom to it—it scared me to death. I was so frightened. I realized how hard I've been, how wrong, how rebellious.

"But at the same time, it was like God wrapped His arms around me and held me tight. He kept me from sliding any farther as He said, 'I still love you.'

"Daddy, tell me the truth. Who was praying for me Tuesday night?"

I looked into her bloodshot eyes, and once again I recognized the daughter we had raised.

Chrissy's return to the Lord became evident immediately. By that fall, God had opened a miraculous door for her to enroll at a Bible college, where she not only undertook studies but also soon began directing music groups and a large choir, just like her mother. Today she is a pastor's wife in the Midwest with three wonderful children. Through all of this, Carol and I learned as never before that persistent calling upon the Lord breaks through every stronghold of the Devil, for nothing is impossible with God.

For Christians in these troubled times, there is simply no other way.

I will sing of the LORD's great love forever;
   with my mouth I will make your faithfulness
   known throughout all generations.

—Psalm 89:1

Almighty Father, I am in awe of Your faithfulness and the divine power at work in the lives of Your children. I praise You, O Lord, for by Your might and outstretched arm nothing is impossible for You. In times of desperation, help me to remember that You listen when I humbly cry for help and You answer when I call upon Your mighty name. Amen.

Expecting a Miracle

AMY DELOACH, AS TOLD TO CINDY L. HEFLIN

Let us hold unswervingly to the hope we profess,
for he who promised is faithful.

—HEBREWS 10:23

An edgy silence enveloped the darkened room as the radiologist entered quietly, folded his arms, and studied the sonogram of my unborn son. Minutes passed slowly while the monitor's dim glow illuminated a look of concern on the doctor's wrinkled brow. Uneasy, I strained to steal a glimpse of the screen. "Is there a problem with his head?" I asked, shattering the silence.

"No. Everything's fine," he replied flatly, rushing out the door. Although puzzled by the unusual scene, I soon buried any seed of doubt and breathed a sigh of relief. I was grateful for good news. With calm assurance, I patted my expanding tummy, returned to the waiting room, and greeted my husband Scott with a smile. In two brief months, we were joyfully expecting the arrival of our third child.

Life, in fact, had never been better. As Christians, Scott and I felt truly thankful for the abundance of God's blessings! We'd recently celebrated ten wonderful years of marriage, had two precious daughters, and a lovely home. Scott's successful Air Force career even enabled me to stay home with our girls. Still, I couldn't deny the elusive heaviness tugging at my heart. Although I spent time regularly in Bible study and prayer, my spiritual life had grown lukewarm, more a routine than a relationship.

Sunlight streamed across the crowded sanctuary as my family and I arrived for worship the following Sunday. Despite the inviting atmosphere, I felt an intangible emptiness envelope me once again. After slipping into my choir robe, I filed in with the other singers as usual, but while voices filled the air with praise, my restless mind drifted. Searching my heart for answers, I prayed silently, *Please show me your truth, Lord.*

My thoughts refocused as Pastor Lambert presented his message. Like brushstrokes on a canvas, his words created a masterpiece revealing the splendor and majesty of our heavenly Father. Something stirred deep within my heart as I was captivated by the glory of God. As the service closed, I knelt at the altar and recommitted my life to Christ.

The arrival of a new season echoed the joy in my heart as I walked out the front door to my van the following week. Chrysanthemums bursting with color caught my eye while autumn leaves rustled in the crisp morning breeze. Sunlight sparkled through the gold and crimson trees as I drove to the medical center at Offutt Air Force Base for a routine OB appointment. Basking in the peace of God's presence, I sensed that my world was in perfect harmony.

I waited patiently in the exam room, barely noticing the lengthy delay, until the stiff military doctor opened the door. With his eyes glued to my chart, the obstetrician's tone was dry and matter-of-fact. "Of course, they told you what the ultrasound detected. He's hydrocephalic. With the ventricles full of fluid, it's impossible for the brain to develop."

Stunned, I felt my perfect world shattering. Although barely able to suppress my anguish, I rushed to the van and hurried home to call Scott. As I raced through the tree-lined streets, a flood of questions twisted and tangled my thoughts. *Is there any hope for this baby? How could I ever face his death? I just rededicated my life to You, God! Don't You promise to protect believers from harm?*

Because of the severity of our baby's condition, we received an immediate referral off base to perinatalogist Dr. John Riley.* He promptly ordered a series of tests, reviewed my records, and scheduled a consultation. Meanwhile, Scott and I prayed that this nightmare was nothing more than a terrible mistake. After a few sleepless nights, we arrived for our appointment with frazzled nerves but high hopes.

Dr. Riley welcomed us with a smile and invited us into his office to discuss our case. His quiet confidence and reassuring manner soon put me at ease. "I'm very sorry about your situation. Test results do confirm the diagnosis of hydrocephaly," he explained. "However, the cause is undetermined. In fact, the good news is that all of the life-threatening diseases frequently associated with hydrocephaly have been ruled out."

Dr. Riley continued, carefully describing the complications we could expect: mild to severe mental retardation, Downs-related symptoms, heart problems, poor motor skills, and inability to participate in sports. "Unfortunately, there's nothing we can do," he said. "The only option I can offer is—abortion."

Dazed and speechless, I heard Scott's firm response. "No!"

Night and day, I wrestled with reality, struggling to accept the heartbreaking truth. My baby would be born with this birth defect and neither I nor medical science could do anything about it. I sensed God asking, *Will you turn to Me or to the world?* The world offered no hope. I had to depend on God alone and pray for the grace to handle whatever my son might be like.

To conceal our anxiety, Scott and I kept busy with our girls and tried to concentrate on other interests. Scott focused on directing the Thanksgiving play he'd written for our church while I plunged into projects at home. To silence my fearful thoughts, I stencil-painted the bathroom, sewed costumes for the Christmas pageant, and baked oodles of homemade bread for family and friends. "He who began a good work in you will carry it on to completion" (Phil. 1:6), I often reminded myself, but sometimes it was impossible to stifle the pain.

One rainy afternoon while Lauren and Vanessa quietly watched a

---

* Pseudonym.

video, I struggled once again to keep my heartache submerged. Easing into a comfy recliner, I propped my feet up, closed my eyes, and tried to relax but soon grew restless. While a rainstorm rumbled against the roof, I rummaged through Scott's toolbox for hammer and nails to hang a few family photos in the upstairs hall. I spread the pictures across the floor to choose the best arrangement. Surrounded as I was by the smiling faces of loved ones, all of my defenses crumbled. A flood of emotions swept over me as I wondered about my baby. *Who would he look like? What color would his hair be?* Immersed under the pressure, I broke down completely.

Keeping busy helped to pass the time each day, but the nights always seemed harder. After bedtime prayers and goodnight kisses with my precious daughters, our house was quiet. Too quiet. To vanquish the silence and our anxious thoughts, Scott and I found laughter a good medicine. So, each night we snuggled together watching old sitcoms until we fell asleep.

Yet, through it all, God blessed us abundantly. Enveloped in the love and prayers of family and friends, we never walked alone. Our families were a tremendous source of support, always lending a hand, bathing us in prayer, and staying in touch with encouraging calls and cards. Our church family showered us with love. "We see your peace and trust," they often affirmed, as our baby became *their baby,* too. One friend, a reassuring obstetrics nurse, gave us a tour of the Neonatal Intensive Care Unit. Together, we prepared for the worst and prayed for a miracle.

Clinging to the assurance of God's Word each day, I focused less on my fears and more on God's faithfulness. His divine timing always amazed me. Receiving an encouraging card or a comforting Scripture precisely when I most needed it, I learned "God is [my] refuge and strength, an ever-present help in trouble" (Ps. 46:1).

Our trust in God grew stronger. Our peace began to build.

As the weeks passed, Dr. Riley monitored the baby's condition frequently. There were weekly exams and fetal monitoring, biweekly ultrasounds, and a variety of other high-tech diagnostics. Careful scrutiny of the data by the chief radiologist even gave us a little hope. "Fortunately, it's not the worst case scenario," he assured. Still, my OB scheduled an early delivery with surgery soon after to insert a shunt for draining fluid off the baby's brain.

When November finally arrived, I felt assured of Dr. Riley's expertise and confident of God's faithfulness. With the scheduled delivery only one week away, I made yet another trip to the doctor's office for my final ultrasound. By now, the whole procedure seemed routine. Scott and I were ready to receive the final report. The radiology tech set up the equipment, and soon Dr. Riley stepped into the small, dark room to observe the ultrasound. Suddenly he whispered to the technician, pointed at the monitor, and abruptly left the room.

My heart sank once again! Frozen in fear, I held my breath. *What now, Lord Jesus?* I shot a glance across the darkened room at my husband. Scott's jaw was firm as he studied the illuminated screen. Then a familiar half-grin spread knowingly across his face and, looking up, his eyes locked with mine.

Soon, Dr. Riley returned. "Folks, I have no explanation for this," he said. "I contacted my colleague on the East Coast, and *he* has no explanation either. We have never seen or heard of *any* case of hydrocephaly . . . resolving on it's own before birth." Dr. Riley shook his head. "I see it, but I just can't believe it. This is a first!"

"It's the power of prayer!" I cried, my eyes misty.

"Well, whatever you're doing, keep on doing it," he chuckled, shaking his head.

I left the doctor's office beaming with delight. Snowflakes danced in the frosty air as Scott and I strolled arm in arm across the parking lot. He quickly started the van and cranked up the music. "Almighty, Most Holy God! Faithful through the ages . . ." We sang along at the top of our voices all of the way home.

With grateful hearts, we reported the news to our loved ones. Together we rejoiced and praised the Lord for His awesome power!

Two weeks later, our precious son was born—perfectly normal and healthy in every way. What a joy to hold this newborn miracle in my arms! To gaze into his sparkling eyes and behold this beautiful answer to prayer—face to face! We named him Zachary Thomas. We chose Zachary, which means "Jehovah hath remembered our prayers," and Thomas for our doubts.

I'll never forget the look of wonder on Dr. Riley's face when he examined Zachary in the delivery room. For weeks after our son's birth, the puzzled physician carried a photo of our son's abnormal ultrasound in the pocket of his lab coat. At the hospital, he was often seen showing it to others, shaking his head as he mused aloud, "Now, see that fluid right there. . . ."

Several days later, our entire family was present for the performance of Scott's play, "The Thanksgiving Zone." It was Zachary's first outing. With excitement and wonder, our church family gathered around us to see our tiny miracle. One of the members, a doctor of genetics, marveled as he touched Zachary's little head. Another invited him to play baby Jesus in the Christmas pageant.

"What an incredible blessing to see Grandpa DeLoach holding his newborn grandson!" Pastor Lambert exclaimed from the pulpit. "This isn't a medical miracle. It's God's miracle! He can do what medical science cannot do—for all things are possible with God!"

> O Lord, you are my God;
> I will exalt you and praise your name,
> for in perfect faithfulness
> you have done marvelous things.
> —Isaiah 25:1

Prayer

O Father, in awesome wonder I proclaim Your faithfulness and tremendous love at work in my life. When circumstances are beyond my understanding, You faithfully care for me and tenderly carry me through. My joy and gratitude is infinite! My heart will sing of Your steadfast love forever! Amen.

Crossroad on the Curve

JOEY DENTON, AS TOLD TO LINDA J. GILDEN

Though I walk in the midst of trouble,
you preserve my life; you stretch out your hand against the
anger of my foes, with your right hand you save me.

—PSALM 138:7

As the four of us climbed into Hank's truck, our mood was festive, and we joked as we buckled up. Hank and Brenda, our youth counselors, had offered to give me a ride home from church. Abby, their three-year-old daughter, sat next to me.

Although the cab of the truck was small, we didn't mind sitting close together. We had just finished decorating the church dining hall for our Valentine party. The youth hosted this annual event for our senior citizens.

Rounding a particularly bad curve that moonless night, we were startled when another truck came up behind us and passed at a high rate of speed. Hank's only alternative to having his truck sideswiped was to swerve onto the shoulder. As the truck passed, Hank flashed his bright lights at the other fellow. We stopped to ensure that everyone was okay, then pulled back onto the pavement.

"That man should watch where he's going," Brenda commented.

"He ought to be locked up," added Hank. "He's going to hurt somebody if he keeps driving like that."

The driver in front of us suddenly screeched his tires and stopped. He got out and stepped into the road, causing Hank to slam on his brakes.

"Don't you blink your bright lights at me like that. I'll kick your ___." Vulgar language flowed freely from this man's mouth. He smelled strongly of alcohol.

Hank floored the accelerator and started around the man. As we passed within inches of his feet, "Billy Bob," as we nicknamed him, punched our truck with his fist.

"Good-bye, Billy Bob," said Brenda as we put welcome distance between him and us.

Looking in the rearview mirror, Hank exclaimed, "Oh, no!"

Billy Bob's truck once again zoomed in our direction. Smoke billowed as the rapid acceleration burned rubber from his tires. In seconds, his truck pulled up alongside ours. His menacing expression matched that of his friend in the seat beside him.

Flooring the gas pedal, Billy Bob sped past us and spun his truck around as a roadblock. "Hold on," cried Hank as he went around him again. My knuckles turned white as I gripped the edge of the seat. My heart pounded with fear and my teeth seemed glued together.

Hank said, "The road is really desolate up ahead. I think we'd be safer if we went back the other way. I'm going to turn around at that Volunteer Fire Department." Hank quickly passed Billy Bob's truck and turned into the parking lot of the fire department.

Hank paused for one quick look to ensure that no other vehicle was coming in the other lane. That was one quick look too long! Billy Bob quickly moved his truck to block ours, then got out again.

Seconds later, our windshield exploded violently, glass shards covering each of us. The brightest fireball of light I had ever seen blinded me. My hands instinctively covered my face. That split second seemed an eternity.

Slowly I moved my hands down my face. Something warm and sticky was all over me. Certain I had been shot, I opened my eyes. I could see! Feeling no physical pain, I realized that I was not hurt.

I turned toward Hank. He was staring at Brenda with the most horrified expression I have ever seen. Fearfully, I looked at Brenda. Blood poured out of both sides of her face at once. One side was inflamed and already swollen to the size of a grapefruit. Pain lifted her screams to unbelievable levels.

Huddled on the floor of the small truck, Abby began to whimper. Instinctively, I covered her with my upper body in case the attack was not over.

Please, God, help us! My simple silent prayer was the most sincere I'd ever offered.

Billy Bob ran to our truck, holding his gun in front of him. "You don't mess with me. You're gonna have to learn that real fast." He began to beat the hood of the truck with the butt of his gun.

Hank reached his hand out of his window and tried to grab the barrel of the gun, desperate to protect his family. "Leave us alone, man. Can't you see you've shot my wife? I need to get her to a hospital," Hank pleaded with this monster of a man.

"I'm gonna kill all of you."

I reached down to ensure that I was protecting Abby. Raising my head, I looked squarely down the barrel of Billy Bob's shotgun.

"God, please help me!" I cried.

Click! I stiffened with fear. It took a few seconds before I realized that the *click* had not been followed by the normal sound of an exploding shell. Billy Bob's gun had only one shell, and it was already spent!

Realizing that his weapon was no longer useful, Billy Bob ran back to his truck and started the engine. He and his friend sped away.

Immediately, I ran into the fire department. Two firemen looked up from their card game, shocked to see a teenager covered with blood.

"We've been shot!" I yelled, approaching hysteria. "Help us!"

Springing into action, the firemen began to take care of our physical needs. The ambulance arrived to take Brenda to the hospital. Police officers came and began asking questions. Suddenly my parents appeared, surrounding us with love and support.

After that terrifying night, none of us will ever be the same. Brenda's physical scars are a constant reminder to us. Our emotional scars have taken even longer to heal.

My faith had never been put to such a test as when I looked down the barrel of Billy Bob's weapon. I will never forget the face at the other end of that shotgun. But neither will I forget the Face of the Faithful One on the other end of my prayers who gave me strength for that night. And I think I will always remember—"When I am afraid, I will trust in you"(Psalm 56:3).

> In God I trust; I will not be afraid.
>   What can mortal man do to me?
> I am under vows to you, O God;
>   I will present my thank offerings to you.
> For you have delivered me from death
>   and my feet from stumbling,
> that I may walk before God
>   in the light of life.
>   —Psalm 56:4, 12–13

Prayer

O Lord, my God, I am in awe of You! Your love and faithfulness to me are beyond measure. You, O Lord, are my light and my salvation, whom shall I fear? You are the strength of my life; of whom shall I be afraid? Though the wicked rise against me, in You alone shall I be confident all the days of my life. Amen.

Tested by Fire

Norma Blackstock

He will cover you with his wings;
you will be safe in his care;
his faithfulness will protect
and defend you.

—Psalm 91:4 TEV

I'll never forget the morning of July 21, 1999. After seeing my husband off to work, I went back to bed because I hadn't slept well the night before. I woke the second time at 10:30 A.M. and sleepily made my way to the kitchen. On my way, I noticed smoke coming from the utility room. I cracked the door, and huge flames shot out at me.

Petrified, I slammed the door and ran to the bathroom, where the only other person at home, my twenty-one-year-old son, Jason, was getting ready for a day of classes at the local university. "The house is on fire!" I hollered. "Get out, get out!" He jumped out of the shower, pulled on some clothes, and rushed to the blaze. He tried to extinguish the flames with a garden hose, but they were spreading too rapidly.

Meanwhile, I ran to the bedroom to call 911, foolishly making the call from inside instead of outside my home. I was consumed with the devastating possibility of losing our house. We'd bought it brand new eleven years earlier and had redecorated with new carpet, paint, and wall coverings just a couple of years ago. It was even lovelier than when we first bought it, and I was desperate to save it.

Jason, realizing that he couldn't put out the fire that was now burning strongly in the kitchen, had exited the house and thought that I'd done the same. When I entered the main hallway, thick black smoke engulfed me, making it hard to breathe. Everything was pitch black, and smoke got in my eyes, ears, and nostrils. I didn't realize that the fire and smoke would travel so quickly. Because our bedroom was at the opposite end of the house, I'd thought that I had enough time to make the call and get out safely. But I was wrong.

Panicked, I groped my way blindly to the front door. I found the door, but, to my horror, I couldn't find the knob and lock. By now Jason realized I was still in the house, and I heard him outside screaming, "Mama, get out! Get out! Turn the lock!" As I hollered back to him that I couldn't find it, smoke filled my mouth. I felt as though I was on fire—the burning, searing pain inside my lungs was unbearable!

Disoriented and confused, I frantically started back toward the bedroom, planning to knock out a window to try to escape. Halfway there, I realized that I'd die from smoke inhalation before I could get out that way, so I headed back to the front door. Once back in the foyer, I started to pass out. I knew that the flames were close, and I was filled with terror and pain.

As I struggled to maintain consciousness, I silently pleaded to God, *Please help me get out!* Thankfully, I didn't pass out. He gave me fresh strength, and I hurried to the door. Miraculously, He placed my hand on the lock and thrust me suddenly from darkness to light. In that instant, my life was spared.

As soon as Jason saw me, he was beside himself with relief and joy. The firemen hadn't arrived, so my next-door neighbor Lillian took me into her home. As I lay on her living room couch, crying, coughing, and sputtering, she and a few other neighbors lovingly comforted me, called my husband, and attempted to clean my soot-covered body.

Finally, after what seemed like an eternity, the firemen and paramedics arrived. With great care, they checked me out, gave me oxygen, and told me that I must go to the hospital. My husband, Tommy, arrived and was relieved to see that both Jason and I were safe. Brenda, one of my dear church friends who lived close by, offered to take me to the hospital so Tommy could stay at the house while the firefighters were still there. They'd finally managed to put the fire out, but they still had to pack up their gear.

Before we left for the hospital, Tommy told me that the front part of our one-story house was damaged badly. Everything in the utility room was destroyed. The fuse box was fried, the washer and dryer were partially melted, and a huge hole was burned in the middle of the floor. The kitchen also was ruined; the cabinets were melted, the appliances were destroyed, water was standing on the floor, and everything was covered in soot. The living room, dining room, and foyer were badly burned also.

When I arrived at the emergency room, the doctors were very concerned about me. They gave me oxygen and also tested and treated me for carbon monoxide poisoning. The nurses and the doctors told me that I was lucky to be alive. I replied to each one the same, "Luck had nothing to do with it; God spared my life."

Clearly God had protected me because not a single burn mark was on my body. God's promise in Isaiah 43:1–3 became real to me that day:

> Fear not, for I have redeemed you; I have summoned you by name; you are mine. When you pass through the waters, I will be with you; and when you pass through the rivers, they will not sweep over you. When you walk through the fire, you will not be burned; the flames will not set you ablaze. For I am the LORD, your God, the Holy One of Israel, your Savior.

My throat and chest were so raw from the smoke that I'd inhaled that it hurt to talk or eat for the next few weeks, and my bronchial tubes became infected. But I was thankful—it could have been much worse.

When I arrived home five hours later, my children and husband met me with bad news. While I was gone, the house had caught fire again. Unbeknown to the firefighters, the fire had been simmering inside the walls. Upon reaching the attic, the fire burst out over the entire house. Everything was gone but the outer walls and the porches. I started crying. My beloved home that once held many precious memories was destroyed. It felt as though I'd lost part of my family; I was heartbroken.

As the firemen prepared to leave, one of them told me how sorry he was that they weren't able to save my home. He'd even tried to carry out the large, framed senior pictures of each of my four children, but they were already damaged. It meant a lot to me to know how much he cared. After being trapped in a burning house and experiencing the searing heat and risks involved, I'll be forever grateful for those courageous public servants.

As I walked through my house, I couldn't believe my eyes. Several hours earlier, it had been beautiful; now it was ugly and devastated. Parts of the ceiling had fallen in, big holes were in the roof, soaking-wet insulation lay everywhere, pieces of sheetrock were scattered, and wallpaper had peeled off. The appliances and cabinets had started to melt, and our furniture was completely ruined. Many of our things had burned, and what hadn't burned was ruined by smoke, water, and the big globs of black ash that covered everything.

We'd lost everything; nothing was salvageable. It felt strange to own nothing but our cars and the clothes on our backs.

That evening, Brenda graciously took us to her home, cooked us dinner, gave us clean clothes, and fielded phone calls. She became the hands of God to us. Many friends and church members came by to offer their condolences. Through my tears, I quoted aloud Romans 8:28, "And we know that in all things God works for the good of those who love him." These words gave me comfort and peace.

Soon after, we learned that a faulty extension cord connected to the microwave caused the fire. The microwave was sitting on a cabinet next to the utility room door, and the cord ran under that door to the plug. Chemicals and clothing that were nearby had fueled the fire.

It's a terrible feeling to lose virtually everything you own. It was hardest to lose sentimental items, such as our children's wedding portraits, my wedding gown, videotapes of my children and grandchildren, the tape of the first sermon our son preached, and heirlooms from my grandmother and great-aunt. Insurance can't replace such things.

The insurance agents were compassionate and caring, helping us as much as they could. They came the evening of the fire to assess the damage and immediately went to work on our claim. We stayed with family a couple of nights, then the insurance company put us up at a hotel for a week. After that, they rented us a furnished apartment, where we lived for six months while our house was rebuilt. We received a limited amount of money for necessities. It didn't cover all of our needs, but family, friends, and church members gave items and money to help us during this difficult time. To receive the rest of our insurance money, we were required to list every single item that we'd lost, the year we bought it, where we bought it, whether it was a gift, the price paid when it was purchased, and the current cost. This was extremely difficult and time-consuming.

Every time I turned into the driveway, my eyes filled with tears at the sight of our once lovely home reduced to dark, ugly ashes. I felt God's peace and comfort, but I still went through a grieving period. As we started rebuilding our home with our insurance money, Tommy and I prayed for God to give us "beauty for ashes." The money enabled us to buy new furniture, new appliances, and new furnishings. Our home was pretty before the fire, but now it's beautiful. God gave back to us greater than what we had before. We were even able to purchase our first computer which we'd needed for the Bible studies I write and teach.

God has tangibly demonstrated the promise of Isaiah 61:2–3 to our family:

> . . . to comfort all who mourn, and provide for those who grieve in Zion—to bestow on them a crown of beauty instead of ashes, the oil of gladness instead of mourning, and a garment of praise instead of a spirit of despair.

I'm sure that sometime I'll walk through the fiery furnace of affliction again. It might not be a house fire, but there will always be tragedies, disappointments, and setbacks in life. At times, it feels as though the scorching flames will consume me, but I take heart. I know that God's watching. He delights in taking the ugly, charred ashes of life and transforming them into crowns of beauty for His glory.

How good it is to give thanks to you, O Lord,
to sing in your honor, O Most High God,
to proclaim your constant love every morning
and your faithfulness every night.
—Psalm 92:1–2 TEV

Prayer

O God, You are my God! Great is Your faithfulness to protect me from the flames and scorching heat when I pass through life's fiery trials. Although they threaten to destroy me, I will not be burned. You, O Lord, are my comfort and strength! I am safe beneath the shadow of Your wings. In Your name, I lift my hands to praise and worship You! Amen.

PART 2

EXPERIENCE HIS POWER

*God Is All Powerful—He Can Help
Me with Anything*

6

The Magazines

BETH MOORE

The word of God is living and powerful,
and sharper than any two-edged sword.

—HEBREWS 4:12 NKJV

If we adults think that the pressures of the world are almost unbearable, we don't have a clue. Most of us have enough years on us to recognize that we're spinning out of control, to locate the negative power source, and to pull the plug on the treadmill if we're serious enough about changing. I am completely convinced, however, that Satan has launched a full-scale attack on our young people that is so shrewd, powerful, and encompassing that they don't even know what has hit them.

I was painfully reminded of one dimension of this attack recently when I came across a stack of old-fashioned magazines. Not all feathers left in our nests provoke happy memories. One of the things I like best about God, however, is that He can redeem absolutely *anything.* The family memory I want to share in this reflection is not pleasant. I choose to share it because it's *important.* Although I can't say that I'm necessarily glad to have had this feather in my nest, I wouldn't trade the precious little sparrow that left it there for anything in the world. Furthermore, I wouldn't trade what God redeemed out of this one "feather" for a whole handful of happier ones.

I am alarmed about our young people. I wish I could say that my alarm has come strictly from what I've seen and heard through my travels, but that's not true. Although what I've seen "out there" among our youth would be enough to scare a soul half to death, I know more than I ever wanted to know *firsthand*. Satan came calling for my own children. He wanted not only to disable any potential they had to make his life miserable but also to get to their parents. Satan knows that one of the most effective ways to get to any of us in ministry is to get to our children. He got my attention all right. Then *God* got my attention. The Devil didn't get the full victory he wanted in those battles, but neither the girls nor I would mind telling you that he left them pretty bloody.

Satan tailors his schemes to fit his subject; therefore, my girls' battles took on different forms. Amanda discovered the vivid reality of Jesus Christ through her own personal difficulties. Thankfully, Satan never got far enough with her to threaten her life. But I want to share a little bit about Melissa's battle because hers had the potential to be deadly. *Yes,* I mean that it literally could have killed her. She is just one of untold thousands of otherwise sound-thinking, successful Christian young women who have fallen into this life-threatening brand of satanic snare. Melissa is very vocal about her experience and passionately desires that Satan be exposed, and I have not only her permission but also her encouragement to share this.

I'm going to allow Melissa to share her own story through an excerpt from a paper she wrote for one of her college classes. She is one of the gutsiest young women I've ever met, willing to let herself look weak so that God's strength can be revealed and the Devil can be defeated.

It was homecoming, the biggest event of the year for a high-school girl. I was getting ready for the football game. This particular year I was up for homecoming queen, and my dad was there to escort me down the football field. The four other girls and I were anxiously waiting for the life-or-death call.

I had on a Georgiou suit for the occasion and a very expensive formal for the dance. I had an appointment with a makeup artist and manicurist before the dance. I had spent tons of money at a tanning salon hoping that the tanning beds could make me look better. I was the size that I wanted to be due to the fact that I had not eaten in months. I was everything that Hollywood was telling me that I had to be. I was deathly skinny, popular, and completely miserable.

The morning after the event was over, I woke up to the smell of warm blueberry muffins. I walked downstairs only to see the norm. My mom was sitting in the dining room doing her "quiet time." Her "quiet time" was the time she spent alone with God each day. Without catching her attention, I watched her. She was in her old, faded pink robe. Her hair was a mess, and she did not have on a hint of makeup, but she looked so beautiful.

I had watched her do her "quiet time" for seventeen years, but it had never caught my attention like this. There was something about that day that was absolutely brilliant. Her face was radiant. I saw her sitting there in her chair and knew that she was truly satisfied. I wanted what she had. She was confident about who she was, even without makeup on. I envied her. I wanted to have whatever it was that fulfilled her.

I tiptoed up the stairs and dug around in my drawers. Finally, I found my own dusty Bible I had shoved in the drawer every Sunday after church. As I cracked open the Bible, I felt immediate renewal. I felt that I had some kind of energy somewhere deep inside my soul. I flipped through the pages and read words that I did not understand. But I knew that they meant something powerful. I could feel the power. I remember staring at a verse that told me who I was in Christ. It said that my body was not my own and that my body was the temple of the Holy Spirit. I found that my identity was in Christ, Himself. That was refreshing to me, because I hated myself.

I looked up from the pages of the Bible to the walls that surrounded me. I felt instant oppression. The walls were covered with magazine cutouts of Elizabeth Hurley and Kate Moss. The walls were overlapped with pictures of women that resembled skeletons. I tacked these on my walls to remind myself that I was forbidden to eat and that I was fat. I would not pass the pictures without a deep feeling of worthlessness and shame.

A few minutes later I heard my mom walking up the stairs. She said, "Melissa where are you? What are you doing?" The tears streamed down my face. She wrapped me up in her arms and read me the words of King David in Psalms. The words gently soothed my ears and my heart. One by one, my mom and I ripped off the magazine pictures. I bitterly threw the pictures in the trash and walked away in agony. I spent the rest of the day trying to differentiate between who the world wanted me to be and who God wanted me to be. I sat at the computer and typed out Scripture and printed it out. I replaced the bare walls with God's Word. . . .

It was a parent's worst nightmare, and it barreled out of control so fast that our heads were left spinning. Melissa was not a troubled child. She was a deeply loved, very well-adjusted child who had received countless accolades for her successes in all sorts of areas. She was a darling size 6 who couldn't have cared less how many French fries she ate. Then suddenly, through a toxic cocktail of just the right conditions, her little world started quaking. The first I realized the pressure that girls her age were under was a year or so earlier when I took both her and her sister to a nice mall in Houston to try on prom dresses. I took two completely happy, well-adjusted size 6 daughters into the mall, and two hours later left with two terribly depressed teenagers who were convinced that they were fat and ugly. I was so mortified over the mannequins in the windows that I finally checked the dress size on one of them. It was a 2. The girls seemed to forget the trauma over the next few days, but I never could get the experience out of my head. A red flag started waving, but I also knew that I had to be careful not to overreact or over control them.

Time passed without any real signs of oncoming trouble. Melissa had quite an eye for putting clothes together and had decided that she wanted to be a fashion design major when she entered college. She began looking through more and more fashion magazines. I grew concerned and started dialoguing with her about them immediately. I always had to be careful about how I dealt with Melissa. She was the type of child who could have knee-jerked with total rebellion if we forbade her every single potential hazard. Her weight and her attitude remained steady and visibly unaffected, so I just continued to watch and pray. Then something unforeseeable happened.

About two months before the events she described in her paper, someone very dear to Melissa moved literally to the other side of the world. She was absolutely heartbroken. Melissa is much like her mother in that she doesn't just love with her heart. She seems to love with her whole being, so when she gets hurt, she hurts all over—heart, soul, mind, and body. With indescribable alarm, Keith and I began to watch our gregarious child sink under a cloak of despair. The lower her spirits sank, the less appetite she had. Soon everything made her sick to her stomach. Weight began rolling off of her like snow melting under a sudden summer sun.

We immediately took her to doctor after doctor. We never could get a physician to diagnose her with what we suspected. Each one independently diagnosed that she was depressed over the difficult losses she had suffered over the recent years. Her brother had returned to his birth mother, her cherished grandmother had died, and her big sister had gone to college. They each felt that her friend's departure had triggered a full-scale physical, emotional, and mental response to the cumulative losses. Keith and I concurred with their diagnosis, but we also felt that it was leading to an eating disorder with a potential much deadlier result than depression.

Here is the mind-blowing part of this scenario. While we were trying to tell Melissa how sick her precious little body was and how it was starving for food, her peers were telling her how fabulous she looked. I cannot estimate the amount of praise she received for being physically ill. Our precious young people have been totally brainwashed by the media. Pictures on magazine covers that have been doctored and air-brushed to look utterly perfect have become their ideal. How in heaven's name have we been talked into buying "perfectionism" from such a grossly imperfect world?

In one form or another, it's happened to all of us. The difference is that our children are too young to fight it off for themselves. They need our help. And not just from their parents. They need the help of the educated, joyful, trustworthy, and Christ-confident adult believers who will expose the lies and tell them truth. Although many of them may choose not to listen, God will hold us, as the adults of this generation, responsible to tell!

I urge you not to think for a single moment that I have become an expert on dealing with teenage depression or eating disorders. *I have not.* I would advise anyone in the same frightening situation to do the same thing we did: mobilize and seek sound, godly counsel and proper medical attention. I am far from an expert on eating disorders, but I have learned a few things about warfare in my time. Keith and I chose good doctors and counselors and let them do their job. *Then we did our job.* We fought our heads off in prayer and drew our swords like crazy, battling the enemy with the Word of God. In the power of Jesus' name, we absolutely refused Satan any right to destroy our daughter's life.

Thank goodness, we had Melissa's cooperation! She wanted to get better. She did not want to be captive to a stronghold and, to the glory of God, the child did practically everything we asked her. You see, no matter how Keith and I loved her and fought for her, a measure of the battle was hers alone to fight. We could teach her how and support her in prayer, but we couldn't "make her" do what the furious battle demanded.

Many of the Scripture passages in the chapter of *Praying God's Word* called "Overcoming Food-Related Strongholds" were those we prayed over her and she prayed over herself.[1] She used them so much I had to laminate them. I believe that a key to the victory God soon had in her came from her willingness to forsake her pride. I gave her a list of Scriptures that I had personalized by inserting her name in them and instructed her to pray them every day. I never in a million years expected the child to take them to high school with her! I would have thought that she would have been too afraid someone would discover them. Not only was she unafraid of being "discovered" but also she came home to me one day and said, "Mom, I'm going to need a new set of Scriptures. I shared mine with a friend at school who needs them so badly."

When Melissa pulled down the pictures of the bone-thin models and replaced them with Scripture, she was unknowingly performing a vivid demonstration of 2 Corinthians 10:5: "We demolish arguments and every pretension that sets itself up against the knowledge of God, and we take captive every thought to make it obedient to Christ." She tore down their pretension of perfection and the arguments they raised against the truth of God's Word.

Those magazine pictures said something to Melissa contrary to what God says about her. When she tore them down and replaced them with the knowledge of God, she demonstrated in physical terms what we're to do in spiritual terms: take our thoughts captive and make them obedient to Christ. If she had stopped with the physical demonstration, little would have changed. Instead, she began to practice spiritually what she had done physically. She started allowing God's Word to expose the lies she had believed, and she began writing down and believing what He said about her instead. The change didn't come overnight. Change in habitual thinking rarely does. But God used the process of time to do far more than an instant healing would have accomplished. She learned to trust Him, love Him, and depend on Him.

That's when the most amazing thing of all happened. The little that Melissa knew about God and His Word started whetting an appetite in her that she couldn't quench. She pleaded with me to tell her how I came to love Him. She asked me questions about His Word constantly. She studied portions of Scripture, then asked me to listen to her thoughts on it to see if she was interpreting it correctly. She got into in-depth Bible study and went through *Breaking Free* with a group of college girls.[2] Her thirst for God began with desperation but developed into delight—just like her mother's did. And just as it did for thousands of others who have been captured by the healing heart of God.

David was one of those. Psalm 18 is a testimony of his love for God. It is the only psalm David began with the words "I love you, O Lord, my strength" (v. 1), as if bursting at the seams to testify. To me, his approach seems to suggest that he couldn't wait to work up to a crescendo. The psalm literally began with his compulsory confession of intimate affection. Because of my own experience, I have no trouble imagining why David loved God so much. The words immediately following his outburst of love say volumes:

> The Lord is my rock, my fortress and my deliverer;
>> My God is my rock, in whom I take refuge.
>> He is my shield and the horn of my salvation, my
>> stronghold.
>>> —Psalm 18:2

Somewhere along the way, the God of the universe—his father's God, and his grandfather's God—had truly become *his*. Their relationship became deeply intimate in a spiritual sense, somewhat like the two described in the Song of Songs: "I am my beloved's, and my beloved is mine" (Song 6:3 KJV).

I watched the same thing happen to Melissa. God was no longer just her mother's intimate partner. He became *hers*. How? Perhaps David said it well for both of them in the very same psalm:

> He reached down from on high and took hold of me;
>> he drew me out of deep waters.
> He rescued me from my powerful enemy,
>> from my foes, who were too strong for me.
> They confronted me in the day of my disaster
>> [in other words, they took advantage of David's
>> weakened state, just as the enemy took advantage
>> of Melissa's after her loss],
>> but the Lord was my support.
> He brought me out into a spacious place;
>> he rescued me because he delighted in me.
>>> —Psalm 18:16–19

I have watched God perform a staggering miracle. Before my very eyes, over the course of a year, He took her disaster and used it to teach her delight.

Her lessons in passion still continue today. No, I don't know about tomorrow, but I have to believe that what she learned in her "yesterdays" will help draw her home in her "tomorrows." Melissa is a very young woman and has plenty of battles in front of her, but she has a victory behind her that sent Satan into a tailspin. For now, the child is head over heels in love with Jesus. Her Bible looks like it's been through the dishwasher. Melissa knows where she's "been had" and has to live on her guard constantly. She may be vulnerable to the same attack for many years, but at her young age she has encountered a God more alive, active, and powerful than she ever imagined.

Teach me your way, O Lord,
 and I will walk in your truth; . . .
I will praise you, O Lord my God, with all my heart;
 I will glorify your name forever.
—Psalm 86:11–12

Lord Jesus, how priceless to me is the power of Your Truth! With humility and gratitude I worship You! For Your Word is alive and active in me, and full of divine power to demolish every stronghold in my life. I praise You, my Redeemer, for empowering me to triumph victoriously over the evil one! My joy in You is everlasting! Amen.

The Unexpected Journey

LISA WEEKS, AS TOLD TO CINDY L. HEFLIN

My grace is sufficient for you,
for my power is made perfect in weakness.

−2 CORINTHIANS 12:9

Ready for a week of rest and relaxation, my husband John and I left the pressures of the working world behind as we pulled onto the interstate and headed south. A vacation at the beach seemed the perfect solace for dreaming together of precious days to come. John and I were expecting our first child, due in three months!

Our prayers finally answered; we were excited and hopeful, filled with all of the joys that expectant parents experience: hearing the heartbeat for the first time, seeing the initial sonogram image, and all of the miraculous wonders of being pregnant. We felt truly blessed! Like the road ahead, blue skies and sunshine spanned the horizon before us.

After driving several hours, we stopped for dinner. But as we traveled on to Asheville, North Carolina, to stay overnight, I began feeling strangely uncomfortable. I'd never been pregnant before, but being an RN, I sensed that something wasn't quite right. *An upset stomach and a backache—probably a bladder infection,* I thought. We journeyed on.

Once at our hotel, I tried to sleep. Symptoms persisted then suddenly grew worse. At 2:30 A.M., I was alarmed to discover bleeding and woke John immediately. He calmly helped me back to bed—then fell apart.

The nurse in me took charge. "I *think* there's a hospital in town that delivers babies," the front desk clerk guessed. Can you imagine our anxiety? We were three hundred miles from home. We knew nothing about Asheville, North Carolina, and weren't even sure there was a hospital in town that delivered babies. These were anxious moments.

The bleeding continued. I wasn't sure what to think. I'm no OB nurse, but I knew something was wrong—but what? I called the nearest hospital.

"Sounds like a bladder infection," said the resident on call. "Having any contractions?"

"I'm not sure what contractions are like, but my back hurts and my stomach's queasy."

"Come in tonight, or wait until morning—whichever you prefer."

I hung up the phone. John said, "Let's go!"

With a map drawn by the desk clerk, John deciphered the route to Mission Memorial Hospital through the dark, unfamiliar city while I lay on the back seat, moaning with ever-increasing pain. When we arrived, an orderly wheeled me to labor and delivery. Believing I had a bladder infection, they ordered lab tests and waited for the results. Around 4:30 A.M., the doctor decided to do a pelvic exam. I will never forget his exact words.

"My. Oh, my. Oh, my goodness!"

I knew little about obstetrics, but this was probably *not* a good sign.

"You're four to five centimeters dilated. And I think I feel the baby's hands."

I began crying. I knew four to five centimeters was halfway to delivery. Being only twenty-six weeks pregnant, I knew that this was horrible. My brain went numb. *What a terrible situation,* I thought. Then it registered. *Oh! This is happening to me, and John, and our baby!*

John went pale. "I think I'm going to be sick."

You can't pass out! You're the only one in this city or state I know!

The doctor ordered an ultrasound and started IV drugs to stop the labor process. Despite the medications, contractions continued. Intensity increased. Completely unprepared, I had no idea what to expect. We hadn't even taken childbirth classes yet.

By 6:30 A.M., it was too late.

After receiving a spinal, they prepped me for a C-section. A throng of nurses and specialists assembled. The atmosphere in the delivery room was tense. Terrifying. But John was by my side.

At 7:03 A.M., Katlin Danae arrived, weighing 2 pounds 6 ounces.

We barely caught a glimpse as they whisked our daughter to the neonatal intensive care unit. John checked on her frequently. He asked the nurse, "On a scale of one-to-ten, ten being the worst child you've taken care of, where would Katlin fit in?"

"Eight or nine."

Our baby was extremely ill.

As soon as I could sit up, John wheeled me to the nursery. Seeing my baby at last, took my breath away. She was perfectly formed and delicate, yet tiny. Fragile. Skin so transparent you could almost see right through it. With tubes, monitors and equipment sustaining her life, it all seemed unreal. I felt a fear of loss, a fear of getting attached—uncertain if she would survive.

But God was in control.

Mission Memorial Hospital, we soon learned, had the highest-rated neonatal intensive care unit in the state. Under the expertise of the neonatologist, Katlin was the first infant to benefit from an advanced surfactant treatment developed to stimulate premature lungs before the first breath of life. Though scared and alone in a strange city, we soon realized that God had directed us to Mission Memorial.

My parents arrived the following day. Going through the details was emotional. This was their first grandchild.

"After John called about the baby," Mama told us, "we phoned the pastor." Word spread quickly. As family and friends nationwide prayed on our behalf, the panic in my heart subsided and God saturated me with His peace.

Still, I longed to be with Katlin every minute I could. Night and day, John and I sat in the NICU watching over our child, a tiny being attached to IVs, monitors, and a ventilator. We realized that many babies born early don't make it, and many who do aren't blessed with good health. The journey ahead would require a strength greater than our own.

My grace is sufficient for you, for my power is made perfect in weakness. I'd learned this Scripture long ago. Now I would learn to rely on it.

Like a roller-coaster ride in the dark, Katlin's battle for life had many ups, downs, and looming uncertainties. On her fourth day of life, she was taken off the ventilator, miraculously able to breathe on her own. But other problems developed. Her condition remained unstable. Her weight plunged to 1 pound 13 ounces. One day, the nurses dressed her in the bonnet and gown from a little doll my parents had given her. It was unbelievable.

Day by day, God demonstrated that His grace and power were truly sufficient.

Just before I was released from the hospital, a caring staff member introduced us to a special couple. Bill and Joanne Biddle also had a baby born three months prematurely. He was now a happy, healthy seven-year-old. Blessed abundantly, they'd often prayed for an opportunity to help another couple. What comfort and encouragement we received from their visit!

The following day, Joanne returned. "Since you'll be in Asheville a few months," she said. "Bill and I want to help." She invited us to stay in their home—free of charge—until Katlin could leave the hospital. "We're leaving for vacation," she continued. "Your parents are welcome to stay with you while we're gone."

John and I were dumbfounded. *This couple doesn't even know us, yet they willingly offer their home?* Consumed with concern for our baby, we'd given no thought to our long-term plans. And we really couldn't afford to stay at a hotel for three months. Gratefully, we praised God for meeting our need before we even recognized it!

The Lord continued to lavish His love upon us in unexpected ways. Through our church in Lexington, Kentucky, word of our plight reached several congregations in Asheville. Although we were strangers in an unfamiliar city, we were soon surrounded by the family of God. Their concern and support left us speechless. Their cards, visits, gifts, food, and prayers encouraged our hearts. "They seem to realize how they'd feel," John said, "if they were in our shoes."

Gradually, Katlin's condition improved. Through a tiny tube in her nose, she began taking my breast milk. Slowly, her weight increased. A mere one-half ounce per day. She remained on antibiotics and IVs, but soon graduated to the step-down unit.

After a while, John needed to return to work in Lexington. Each weekend he made the long trip back. But during the week, the distance of miles and emotions between us was difficult. Both of us were dealing with different challenges. John wanted to be by my side with his strength and support but couldn't. Staying in touch by phone each day, he did his best to encourage me. But he later admitted, "From one report to the next, I worried, *Will this be the setback she doesn't survive?*"

Exhausted and emotionally drained, I'd return from the hospital some days thinking, *I can't go back another day.* The Biddles always listened, encouraged, and prayed with me, providing much more than a place to stay. Still, at times I felt so alone in my pain. Silent questions lay trapped inside my heart. I realized that God had given us this baby, and He alone was in control. Her very life and the course of our future rested in His omnipotent hands.

Our journey continued. Along the way, Katlin experienced numerous setbacks. Being unable to do anything but observe—like a spectator on the sidelines—was frustrating. Stressful. With compassion and kindness, however, the nurses ministered to us as angels in our time of need. Especially Sandy. By sharing her deep faith, she encouraged me often. By virtue of her skill and expertise, she enabled me to focus on being the mom—instead of a nurse concerned about all of the technical details. I always felt reassured when my baby was under Sandy's care.

Slowly, Katlin's growth continued. God performed an incredible miracle before my very eyes. Watching her develop from a preemie into a healthy baby was awesome. Praise God, she suffered no vision loss, hearing problems, brain damage, or other complications common to premature infants. Her body was perfect—just missing the baby fat. Three weeks before her due date, Katlin tipped the scales at five pounds—hefty enough to be released at last!

Overjoyed, John and I praised the Lord for answering our prayers. By His sufficiency and great power, God had met our every need, from the impossible to the insignificant. How awesome and worthy of our adoration He truly is!

John and I were thrilled and a bit nervous to finally bring our precious daughter home. Before leaving the hospital, we received thorough instruction on infant CPR and use of the monitor that Katlin needed because of occasional episodes of apnea. The eight-hour trip back to Lexington seemed to take forever. After ten intense weeks out of town, I could hardly wait to be at home with my baby. What relief I felt as we turned into the driveway of the cutest Cape Cod on Bob-O-Link Drive! By God's grace, our unexpected journey had finally come to an end.

A new one was about to begin.

Praise the LORD.
Give thanks to the LORD, for he is good;
   his love endures forever.
Who can proclaim the mighty acts of the LORD
   or fully declare his praise?

—Psalm 106:1–2

Heavenly Father, in awe and wonder I proclaim Your incomparable power. You alone are the God Most High! How mighty is Your healing touch. With Your omnipotent hand, You create each living being and sustain Your precious little ones. My joy and gratitude are inexpressible, for You have been my refuge and place of safety in the day of my distress. Amen.

8

It Only Takes a Spark

KIM CASON, AS TOLD TO CINDY L. HEFLIN

With man this is impossible,
but with God all things are possible.

—MATTHEW 19:26

Breathing in the serenity of the mountainside retreat, I snuggled next to my husband and closed my eyes. Poplar trees rustled in the early morning breeze while chickadees rendered a sunrise serenade. From our lofty deck, we watched the sun rise slowly above the smoky mist, splashing light upon the majestic peaks nearby. Tranquility soothed our frazzled souls, melting away the tension of the world we'd left behind.

Don and I were the typical American couple: two great kids, two-story home, two demanding careers, and two nonstop schedules. Too busy, in fact, to enjoy life at all. Briefly free from the pressures of fast-forward living, we welcomed the chance to reconnect as a couple and enjoy the beauty of God's creation. Little did we know that our weekend escape to the Great Smoky Mountains would change our lives forever.

The Smokies offered the respite Don and I desperately needed. We hiked sun-dappled trails along sparkling streams, picnicked in the park with a basket of gourmet goodies, and enjoyed breathtaking mountain vistas each evening at sunset. Our getaway soon rekindled our love for the Smokies and our dream of running a motel in the mountains after retirement—in twenty-five years or so.

While the distant future seemed crystal clear, our current circumstances caused waves of restless confusion. Pursuing the American dream, Don and I had little time for family, friends, or even each other. Though successful, our careers and business ventures never delivered the satisfaction they had promised. As our children grew older, work demands increased, placing a strain on us all. I often prayed, seeking God's direction for our family, but His plan was as hazy as the mountain mist.

All too soon, Don loaded our luggage into the minivan, and we headed home. Reluctant to return to the rat race, I gazed in the rearview mirror as the tranquil Smoky Mountains faded into the distance.

During the long drive, we prayed for wisdom. After years of living on overload, I knew God was nudging us to adjust our priorities. Curb our commitments. Downscale. But how? Two-years earlier, I gave up my management position only to battle fears over finances. In desperation, we put our custom-built home on the market *twice* but never received an offer.

Still, the struggle drew us closer to God. Our spiritual growth accelerated when we joined a couples Bible study fellowship and served as activity directors. Learning to walk by faith through trials and opportunities alike, we allowed God to mold us until our lone desire was to seek His will, whatever it might be.

The morning after returning from our trip, Don dashed into the kitchen to grab a cup of coffee before heading to the office. He looked sharp in his power-suit and tie, but his eyes grew narrow and pensive. "Kim?" he asked, thinking out loud. "Why are we waiting until *retirement* to open a place in the mountains? Why don't we do it *now!*"

What? I stared at Don in disbelief. *Could we?*

All morning long, I pushed through piles of paperwork and returned phone calls, trying to concentrate. But Don's words and the lovely bed and breakfast I'd visited on a recent business trip kept running through my mind. *Lord?* I prayed. *Could this be the answer for our family?*

Suddenly, I was a woman with a mission! By day, I tracked down available information on the Smoky Mountain region and the bed-and-breakfast industry. At night, after tucking in the children, Don and I discussed ideas and prayed for direction. I'll never forget the sultry evening my family gathered on my parent's patio. As we shared our dream, they listened with enthusiasm, then prayed for God to bless and guide us.

Several weeks later, we returned to Gatlinburg for a family reunion. While there, we scoured the ads and scouted the area, searching for available real estate. Although the list was slim, Don and I began our excursion, eager to discover God's opportunity for us.

"Needs lots of repair." Don frowned, driving by one bed and breakfast.

We saw another. "Nice. But, too small to generate income."

We ventured on.

Winding along scenic mountain roads, Don and I arrived at another property. We pulled up the gravel drive, and just beyond a thicket of trees I saw a hidden treasure nestled on the wooded mountainside—a charming country inn with an inviting wraparound porch! As the sun peeked over the treetops, illuminating the multigabled two-story, the inn appeared an unpolished gem, but nonetheless, a jewel. At once, I sensed something strangely familiar, like coming home to a place I'd never been.

We followed the walk to the wide, breezy porch where a cluster of rockers beckoned us to "set-a-spell" and savor the beauty of the view. A welcoming entrance invited guests to "Come In!" so I pushed open the door and slipped inside. Pausing at the entry, I gazed about in wonder! Before my eyes a grand staircase reached heavenward, sunlight saturating the balcony above. A spacious gathering room flanked by duplicate stone fireplaces encircled the stairs. Multiple windows lured the beauty of the outside in. Scattered about the expansive room were many cozy nooks—perfect for reading or moments of intimate conversation. French doors overlooking the porch graced the dining room to the right and accented a grand piano to the left.

It was beautifully built, just needed some polish—a decorator's touch—inside and out.

"You don't want a room tonight, do ya?" A gruff voice startled me as a petite gray-haired woman ambled down the stairs.

"Well, we were just interested," I said, smiling. "We heard the inn was for sale."

We introduced ourselves to the innkeeper, Ellen.*

"Look around if you want," she said flatly.

I nearly raced through our self-guided tour. In all, there were nine guest rooms, a lovely bridal suite, a sizable kitchen, and the innkeeper's quarters on the lower level. By the time we completed our tour, thanked the owner, and said good-bye, one thing was certain—we'd fallen in love with the Eight Gables Inn!

"Can you believe it?" I beamed, climbing into the van.

"It's perfect," Don said. "And *way* out of our price range!"

It was hard to admit, but my husband was right. The price tag was nearly double our limit. The odds stacked against us were higher than the Alps. Still, somehow I felt hopeful.

Lord, I prayed, *give me just one reason to believe!*

"It was built three years ago," Don said, listing facts he'd learned from the owner. "She's selling because of health problems. Been on the market awhile, but the realtor's contract just expired."

No realtor fees? Thank you, Jesus! My heart swelled with hope.

The next Sunday, we attended church as usual, but there was nothing ordinary about the message that Don and I heard. We exchanged glances as our pastor spoke on "Facing the Future with Faith" and we were stunned by our Bible teacher's lesson, "Seize the Moment!"

Staggered by God's omnipotence, we agreed, "This is *His* timing. *His* plan!"

Our quest began.

We prayed diligently for wisdom. Don labored for hours each night, developing our business plan. Soon, we were on the road to Gatlinburg again.

Open the way for us, Lord! I prayed silently as Don and I arrived for

---

* Pseudonym.

an appointment at a local bank. With courage, we shared our plans with the loan officer and submitted an application. For extra measure, we applied at two other local banks. The gentleman in charge at the last institution responded favorably. He gave us hope.

Before leaving town, we visited the public school our children would attend. In one classroom, I spotted an open Bible lying on a bookshelf. My eyes grew misty as I sensed God's assurance that He and my children were welcome here.

Greatly encouraged by the trip, Don and I used the long drive home productively. While the children kept busy with games and books, we updated our résumés, wrote a newspaper ad for our home, and listed items we'd need to sell before moving—including our dog, Buffy. We brainstormed ideas to create a Christian bed and breakfast that would refresh, nurture, and minister to our guests at Eight Gables Inn.

It was closing time when we pulled in at the vet, so the kids and I ran in to pick up Buffy. Posted by the desk was a notice: "If interested in selling your dog, please sign below." We all loved Buffy but knew that he couldn't stay with us if we became innkeepers. So I scribbled down our number as the assistant locked up. A woman called the next day and bought the dog.

Our every concern was under God's control. He even provided a new home for Buffy. My faith and peace flourished. Our plans were coming together perfectly, until . . .

The loan officer of the first bank phoned. "Your loan is denied," he said. "You have *no* experience."

With faith and determination, we forged ahead, certain that God was sending us to the mountains for His purpose.

"You have *no* money," the second banker laughed. "It takes ten years to be accepted in this town."

We'll see about that! We didn't give up. One bank remained.

"I lift my eyes to the hills, where does my help come from?" I prayed, reciting a favorite verse as I cleaned house one dreary morning. "My help comes from the Lord!" Suddenly, I felt an incredible peace, as if Jesus were standing right beside me. A familiar tune came to mind. *It only takes a spark* . . . were the few lyrics I could recall.

Kim, you may have only a spark of what it takes to make this work, God spoke to my heart, *but I will do the rest!*

Autumn leaves tumbled in the afternoon drizzle as I rushed out for an errand hours later. Reaching across the dash, I switched on the radio, and the music of my morning filled the van. "I'll shout it from the mountaintops. I want my world to know. I want to pass it on."[1]

Tears stung my eyes. "O Lord, that's where Eight Gables is—the mountains!"

Clinging to God's promise, we waited for the doors to open. The following week they did!

"It's a go," said the loan officer of the remaining bank, "provided you sell your home and secure a loan through the Small Business Administration."

Our home went up for sale immediately.

Eight days later, Don called the bank. "We sold it!"

"Uh, there's been a change," said the banker. "You'll need an additional 10 percent down."

What? Our combined assets barely covered the original minimum down payment. Dejected, Don politely finished the call, then left for a lengthy business trip.

"It's over, Kim!" Don shouted, phoning from the airport. "Another 10 percent? *That's impossible!*"

Unshaken, I set my resolve, determined not to give up. With our home and almost all of our furniture sold, I proceeded as though nothing had changed, knowing that "He who has promised is faithful." Putting my faith into action, I continued preparing for the move. I continued planning menus for the B&B. I continued purchasing Christmas decor for the open house we'd agreed to host to promote the Inn.

In Don's mind, the deal was dead.

Frost glistened on our front porch pumpkins before my husband returned from his trip. Imagine his surprise when he pulled into our driveway.

"Honey?" I asked. "Could you please help Bill load this furniture into his truck? He just bought the bedroom suite."

"What?"

God was still in control!

So Don began dialing for dollars. Night after night, he contacted friends and family, offering them an opportunity to invest in Eight Gables and help us meet our down payment. Progress was slow. With the closing on our home inching ever closer, our goal was still beyond reach.

My hope, once so strong, began ebbing away. My spark of faith was nearly extinguished. Unaware of our predicament, a few friends planned a going away party. As the evening approached, I felt sick with dread. *How can I ever face them?* I wondered. *My home and all of our furniture have been sold—but I'm not going anywhere!*

When the party was only hours away, my friend phoned. Torn between guilt and anxiety, I came clean. "Sorry, I just can't come." I confessed. "I'm *not* moving!"

"Kim," she said. "God's brought you this far—you can't give up now!"

Mustering every ounce of courage within me, I pasted on a beauty pageant smile and rang the doorbell. Surprised by a houseful of friends, I played along, no one the wiser to my secret. An evening of fun and laughter lifted my spirits.

Two days later, a Fed-Ex package from the Small Business Administration arrived at Don's office. In the secretary's absence, his boss picked up the urgent-looking envelope.

"What's this?" he asked, handing Don the delivery.

Noticing the return address, Don rushed to his office, closed the door, and politely phoned our SBA representative. "Please, don't *ever* send personal mail to my office," he said, holding his anger.

"I'm *so* sorry," she apologized. "I thought that was your home address."

"Say," Don asked. "Is it possible to request an additional amount on the loan?"

"We usually don't, but the committee meets tomorrow. How much do you need?"

"Ask for 10 percent. I'll be happy if they agree to 5."

The next afternoon, the conversation long forgotten, Don's phone rang.

"Your additional 10 percent has been approved," said the woman from the SBA.

"Thank you!" Don shouted. "Thank you so much!"

"It's the least I could do after my mistake."

His eyes stung. Amazed by God's power, he thanked the Lord for this huge miracle!

We finalized our moving plans. Two weeks later, my father, a private pilot, flew us to Lexington, Kentucky, for our closing with the SBA. The meeting proceeded smoothly.

After dinner with my parents, we boarded the single-engine Cessna and flew home. It was a cold and windy January night. Several inches of snow covered the ground. Tossed by the wind as it touched down, our plane skidded off the runway, hit a snow bank, and flipped upside down!

By God's omnipotent hand of protection, everyone walked away from the crash. While Mom, Don, and I waited in the car for police and paramedics to arrive, Dad ambled back to the wreckage to retrieve some belongings. The briefcase with our financial documents was battered, its locks torn off from the impact. But everything inside was undisturbed. Everyone was whisked away to the emergency room, treated, and released.

We awoke the next morning sore and bruised but alive. Battling doubts, Don turned to me.

"Maybe God *doesn't* want us to move."

"No. God had many chances to change our situation. We're alive to share this story."

And that's exactly what we did.

Two weeks later, Don and I walked into the perfectly appointed conference room for our closing at the bank. Gathered around a massive table, the finely attired loan officials listened intently as we shared our miracle—how God enabled us to purchase Eight Gables Inn. The stunned expression on the gentlemen's faces reflected an awe for Almighty God that their hearts could not deny.

With Him, a spark of faith can move mountains!

O Sovereign LORD! You have made the heavens and earth by your great power. Nothing is too hard for you!

—Jeremiah 32:17 NLT

Prayer

Almighty God, I bow in humble adoration and marvel at Your mighty power! You direct my path by the same omnipotent hand that placed the earth in motion and spread the stars like a sparkling blanket across the midnight sky. You crush mountains under my feet and with outstretched arms push ocean waves upon the shore. With confidence, I anchor my trust in the Lord Most High! I will proclaim Your praise forever! Amen.

Mom, I'm in Control!

KAREN STRAND

The weapons we fight with are
not the weapons of the world.
On the contrary, they have divine power
to demolish strongholds.

–2 CORINTHIANS 10:4

How do I know you are my mother? State your full name and birth date."

"My name is Karen Christine Strand. I was born on October 17," I replied.

The sight of my teenage son perched on the edge of his hospital bed was nearly more than I could bear. His once-bright brown eyes were clouded with confusion.

"What is wrong with him?" I asked the doctor.

"Jay is suffering from a drug-induced psychosis," the doctor explained. "Not uncommon among those who abuse drugs. It shouldn't last for more than a week." The "week" lasted for two years. Years that would test *and* strengthen my faith in God as no other event in my life **has.**

As a child Jay had been active in church and Sunday school. In high school, he attended home Bible studies. I had no reason to believe that my son was not well-grounded in his Christian faith.

Things changed when he made friends with kids from a nearby school for troubled youth. I thought that Jay had befriended them to tell them about the Lord. Instead, he began questioning his own faith, even experimenting with an Ouija board.

"You know that God forbids fortune-telling and pursuing the occult!" I remonstrated. But he didn't listen. Then my daughter told me that he was smoking pot and using LSD. When I confronted him, he patiently explained that marijuana was a natural nonaddictive herb and that he knew of no one who had been harmed by LSD.

"Trust me, Mom." He smiled. Then, "Mom, I'm in control!"

I was horrified. I cried. I prayed. I grounded him. I left Bible verses on his pillow, had the youth pastor come over, and put him on every prayer chain I knew of. I attended Tough Love meetings. Then Jay turned eighteen and moved out.

When I visited my son's "crash pad" downtown, I saw drawings of skulls with horns and demonic masks taped to the walls. He read books on metaphysics and talked nonsensically about solving the problems of the world. He heard voices. My son was losing it.

The phone call came at 9 A.M. on a Saturday morning. Jay was in jail for assaulting an officer. Jay also thought he was Jesus. When I arrived, he was handcuffed and ready to be transported to the hospital. Wild-eyed, his orange-dyed hair falling over his eyes, he told me there was a .45 magnum in the trunk, and the officers planned to shoot him.

I visited Jay in the psychiatric ward every day. Now he thought the authorities were preventing him from carrying out his special mission from God. Yet in a notebook he wrote, "A demon slipped in and wounded my spirit. Lord, purify me. Save my sanity, O Lord."

My son spent the next two years in and out of the hospital. Between times, he stayed in our home, talking about aliens. When he did not improve, the doctor changed his diagnosis to a "psychosis of undetermined origin." The prognosis was grim.

One morning, desperately searching for help, I reached for my Bible and leafed through the psalms. I wondered why so many of them were about David's enemies. The answer came: *You are not warring against men in armor with swords. But your enemies are just as real. Have you forgotten what it says in Ephesians?*

I opened to Ephesians and read, "Our struggle is not against flesh and blood, but against . . . the powers of this dark world and against the spiritual forces of evil. . . . Put on the full armor of God, so that when the day of evil comes, you may be able to stand your ground" (6:12–13).

Of course. David's enemies were physical, but ours are spiritual! Each day after that, I found psalms about fighting evil and inserted Jay's name where applicable. For example, Psalm 35 became, "Contend, O LORD, with those who contend with [Jay]; fight against those who fight against [Jay]. Take up shield and buckler; arise and come to [Jay's] aid" (vv. 1–2).

Slowly, my son's mind began to clear, and he agreed to have friends come pray for him. So one evening a group of us gathered in the living room. We told Jay about the spiritual warfare we suspected and implored him to confess his rebellion against God and turn his life over to Jesus Christ. Amid a tearful struggle, he did so. Next, accepting our pastor's counsel that his faith must be accompanied by his actions, Jay filled trash bags with psychedelic posters, occult books, heavy metal music tapes, and drug paraphernalia. He destroyed everything in the bags. Another liberating step.

After that, Jay agreed to meet weekly with our associate pastor to study the Bible and learn how to be strong in the Lord. The process continued.

Step by step, Jay's mind was restored. Not because God zapped him with an instant healing or because I had done all the right things, but because of Jay's obedience to what God asked him to do: confess, repent, and be nourished by God's Word. Today my son is a healthy young husband and father of four children, a vibrant Christian who is committed to telling others about his Lord.

To young people today who think that they can safely use drugs or dabble in the occult, I would say, "Watch out! My son thought that, too. But he lost two years of his life before he even knew it was happening."

To other parents of rebellious kids, I offer the two things that helped me most throughout our ordeal. First, determine not to look at the circumstances (which always pulled me down) but to the love, mercy, and power of our Lord to change things. Second, know that if in God's sovereign plan the outcome is not what you pray for, He will still be your constant source of comfort and strength.

God has said, "Never will I leave you; never will I forsake you." So we say with confidence, "The Lord is my helper; I will not be afraid."

—Hebrews 13:5–6

O Lord Most High, I praise Your mighty name! By Your Word, You destroy the spiritual forces of evil in this dark world. By Your matchless power, You release the wayward from the enemy's snare. Thank You, Jesus, for never leaving or forsaking me, even when I turn away from You. How worthy You are of all glory, honor, and praise! Amen.

10

Jar of Clay

CINDY L. HEFLIN

But we have this treasure in jars of clay to show that this
all-surpassing power is from God and not from us.

–2 CORINTHIANS 4:7

With lights flashing and sirens wailing, the ambulance streaked through the early dawn to Central DuPage Hospital. Paramedics burst into the ER, carting a limp, mangled body.

"Cyclist struck by a Jeep!" shouted an EMT. Medics scrambled to connect life-saving equipment to the unconscious young woman. With a single key her sole possession, she arrived as a Jane Doe.

Crushed. Critical. Comatose. Clinging to life by a thread.

But she had so much to live for.

At nearby Wheaton College, the world mission organization TEAM was about to begin the Wednesday morning session of their missionary orientation program. Glancing across the classroom and then at her watch, Karen waited for her roommate to arrive. Like Karen, Dr.

Holly Tapley was eager to complete her training, eager to fulfill God's call on her life to the foreign mission field. It was her destiny.

Holly, firstborn of five, grew up in a Christ-centered family and spent many carefree hours playing in the wooded acres surrounding their Northern Indiana home. An adventurous blonde with a contagious grin, she loved exploring nature, climbing trees, and building forts. Nurtured by the love and training of her parents, Holly claimed Jesus as her Savior at an early age.

And God placed a dream in the young child's heart.

One breezy summer day, seven-year-old Holly stood high on a hill overlooking the house across the street. *I wonder if my neighbors know who Jesus is?* she pondered. *I think I'll go tell 'em! I betcha' there's a lot of people in the world who don't know Jesus. How will they know unless somebody tells them?*

So she left her playmates to "go and tell," curls bouncing along the way.

As Holly grew older, becoming a foreign missionary was always in the back of her mind though never a vocation to which she committed herself.

During high school, she assisted her father, a family practice physician, as a secretary, office nurse, and medical transcriptionist, but she ruled out a career in medicine because she hated the sight of blood. The teen considered the field of psychology, until she discovered that the counseling she desired to do required a master's degree. *Forget grad school! I don't want to go to college for any six years!* She decided to "just get over the blood thing" and become a nurse.

Still, over time, the tug in her heart became impossible to ignore. While a sophomore in college, Holly attended an InterVarsity missions conference that changed the course of her life—forever. As one speaker shared his passion, God captured Holly's heart, clearly confirming His call on her life. In response, she completely committed herself to missions and to following Him—whatever the cost.

As the nursing student prayed for direction, her focus centered on Bangladesh, both because of it's location in the 10-40 window, a region where 95 percent of the world's unevangelized poor live, and because it was the birthplace of her adopted sister, Debby.

"We need nurses desperately," a missionary from Bangladesh told her. "But you *really* should consider medical school. The need for female doctors is great, especially since Muslim beliefs limit the treatment male doctors can give to female patients. It's extremely difficult for women to receive adequate health care."

"I'll pray about it." Holly said, but internally she resisted. *Med school? I went into nursing to avoid grad school!*

Yet, with every tentative step of faith, God seemed to open all the right doors. Holly received a unique exception sparing her an entire year of classes, passed the exam required for medical school applicants after completing only two-thirds of the coursework it tested, and was immediately accepted upon application to Indiana University School of Medicine.

The med student soon discovered that she could receive credit for two months of hospital work in a foreign country and applied for a short-term mission to Bangladesh. The trip didn't work out. Instead, Holly took a two-month assignment to a country in Central Asia. Its culture and people fascinated her; their medical and spiritual needs touched her heart.

With a deep sense of direction and purpose for her life, she returned and soon began her residency. The grueling eighty- to one-hundred-hour-a-week schedule left little time for church, friends, or Christian fellowship. Longing for a "normal" life, Holly began to wonder: *God's call on my life seemed so clear. Did I hear Him right? Could I really go to the mission field and be content as a single?* Suddenly, God's call did not seem so certain.

Holly accepted a second short-term assignment to the Central Asian country that had captured her heart. "When I looked out the window as the plane touched down, a surprising feeling came over me, as if I were coming home. God's blessing of peace, contentment, and excitement for His calling multiplied," she said. "I am reminded of Isaiah 30:21, which says, 'Whether you turn to the right or to the left, your ears will hear a voice behind you, saying, "This is the way, walk in it."' Whenever I've started to wander, even if only in my mind, from the way God has directed, I have, without a doubt, heard His voice guiding me back to His plan of missions."

At last, after years of training, Holly received her medical degree. On the threshold of realizing her dream, she joined Southwestern Medical Clinic and arranged to complete missionary training requirements within a year. In January 2000, Dr. Holly Tapley attended the first session of candidate orientation with the world mission organization TEAM. She returned to Wheaton College for the second session in June.

Rising before dawn, Holly dressed quickly, tiptoed past her roommate Karen, and headed down the steps of Smith Hall dorm, ready to embrace the day ahead. The experienced cyclist often enjoyed a morning ride—a great time for prayer and worship. Holly always felt closer to God when surrounded by nature. Even when "nature" was in the midst of a busy Chicago suburb!

Holly pulled on a windbreaker, fastened her helmet, mounted her blue and gold BMX, and pedaled across campus to the Illinois Prairie Path. After a refreshing ride, she'd soon return with ample time to shower and grab a bite of breakfast before meeting Karen at Blanchard Hall for TEAM's Wednesday morning session.

She should have been here by now. Karen checked her watch again as she waited for her roommate. She tried to focus on the instructor, but as the wall clock ticked, concern for her friend mounted. Karen alerted a staff member and went to Smith dorm to check on her friend. At once, it was obvious—Holly had not returned.

Campus security was notified immediately. Holly had left Smith Hall at 5:15 that morning. It was now 9:30. After double-checking room 304, college officials contacted the Wheaton City police to report a possible missing person.

Police detectives arrived within minutes. With rapid-fire questions, they gathered information quickly. Their concern for "the Jane Doe" at Central DuPage escalating, detectives pressed for a detailed description of Holly. Photo identification confirmed their suspicions. Checking the victim's key, campus security determined a match to **Smith Hall room 304.**

Alarmed by this news, TEAM's Director of New Member Development and his wife rushed to Central DuPage Hospital. They were quietly escorted to the ER for visual identification. Beneath a maze of tubes, monitors, and life support equipment, Holly's slight frame was barely visible. "Jane Doe" was indeed Dr. Holly Tapley!

Crushed. Critical. Comatose. Clinging to life by a thread.

"Police investigators indicate your colleague was crossing a road under construction, when her bicycle was struck by a Jeep Cherokee traveling approximately thirty-five miles per hour," the detective stated. "After impact with the windshield, it's estimated her body was thrown nearly sixty feet before landing on the pavement. She was transported to Central DuPage at about 6:15 A.M."

The couple stood by helplessly while a team of doctors, nurses, and technicians swarmed in and out of the room prepping the patient for surgery. Initial reports were grim.

At the surgery waiting room, TEAM members gathered to pray and wait for news on Holly's condition.

Meanwhile, anxious TEAM staffers struggled to locate Holly's parents. By noon, they reached her father, Dr. Dwight Tapley. He granted TEAM permission to contact Holly's medical practice and sponsoring churches with details of the accident for the purpose of prayer.

Then he phoned Central DuPage.

"Your daughter has sustained extensive trauma and multiple life-threatening injuries," the specialist began. "Severe trauma to the skull . . . Inter-cranial edema . . . C-2 fracture . . . Lower spine fractured twice . . . Dislocated pelvis fractured twice . . . Open fracture of right leg with significant bone loss resulting from exposure to the pavement." He continued. "Bruised kidney . . . Collapsed lung . . . Nearly complete laceration of lower lip . . . Severely fractured jaw . . . Several missing teeth."

Crushed by the devastating report of his daughter's injuries, Dr. Tapley left his office immediately. Anxious to start the two-hour drive to Wheaton, he and his son David waited in the driveway for Mrs. Tapley to return.

"I don't see that she'll still be alive," a Central DuPage physician reported by phone as the Tapleys headed to Wheaton. While David drove, Dwight and Barb prayed, placing their daughter into the heavenly Father's loving care. "Reading Scripture aloud gave us great comfort and assurance of the Lord's deep love," Barb later shared. "The words of Isaiah 61 filled us with a deep sense that He would turn ashes to beauty and bring healing to Holly so she might carry the light of the gospel of Christ to Central Asia."

Upon arrival, the Tapleys rushed to the ICU. Amid tubing, machines, and a pumping ventilator, Holly was comatose—but miraculously *alive!*

"Thank You, Lord Jesus!" they cried, holding each other close.

Solemnly, the lead physician entered the room to brief the family on Holly's case. "Though vitals have stabilized, her condition remains grave," he stated. "The severity of her brain injury, and the permanent damage that may result, is our primary concern." Flipping through the chart, he reported on her numerous critical injuries.

Shock and sorrow silenced Holly's loved ones, but faith and courage calmed their fears. Fervently, they poured out their hearts to the Lord in prayer.

Time staggered by. Dwight and Barb sat silently at their daughter's bedside watching for a glimpse of God's healing power. Occasional eye movement whispered hope. Subtle wiggles of toes and fingers offered a glimmer of promise.

Soon, hundreds of family, friends, and TEAM associates worldwide began receiving prayer requests for Holly via e-mail. As they prayed, God's power became evident.

Within forty-eight hours, the life-threatening pressure on Holly's brain decreased dramatically. Yet, crucial questions remained. Would she ever wake from this coma? Breathe on her own? Will she be completely paralyzed? Suffer permanent brain damage?

Placing their trust in God alone, the Tapleys waited.

The Great Physician demonstrated His healing power. Despite the fracture in Holly's neck, movement was restored to all of her limbs. She awakened from the coma and began breathing on her own. The Tapley family rejoiced!

Gently stroking his daughter's hand, Dwight gave her the devastating news. In a raspy whisper came Holly's first response, "I give it all to Jesus."

Still, the challenges were formidable. Now conscious, the young woman writhed in excruciating pain. Morphine offered some relief, but induced headaches and hallucinations. Her shattered leg and jaw would require further surgery, but the neurologist's report revealed the greatest concern. "Though Holly is responsive and communicating with others, her understanding remains childlike. Confused. No recall. Only time will tell the extent to which these head injury symptoms could persist as permanent brain damage."

Against all odds, the Tapleys pleaded with God to grant complete recovery. Daily reports to their network of praying friends listed specific requests and praised the Lord for Holly's progress. "On the bright side," a family member reported, "Holly knows who her Lord is. Even though she's confused, she prays and says Jesus is helping her."

Steadily, her condition improved. Eight days after doctors doubted that she'd even survive, Holly was transferred out of the ICU! She took several assisted steps, sat up in a chair, and slept through the night. Although pain medication certainly exacerbated her mind's ability to function, Holly's confusion began to lift. One evening, while family and TEAM members gathered by his daughter's bedside, Dwight led the group in prayer. As the last person finished, they were all blessed to hear Holly haltingly offer her own coherent prayer of thanksgiving.

More alert and responsive, Holly worked with a team of doctors, nurses, and therapists daily. Her inner strength and determination amazed them. Progress accelerated. One night, while her sister slept in a chair nearby, Holly pulled out her own feeding tube. "Maybe memory of her medical training is returning!" Family members held firmly to this hope.

Still, problems persisted. Being unable to recall the identity of visitors frustrated and confused Holly. Yet memory of her life-long passion was crystal-clear. "Holly still wants to return to Central Asia," Barb said, "to fulfill the goal she's been preparing for and dreaming of for years."

God's miraculous healing continued. Just seventeen days after the collision, Holly was transferred to a rehabilitation center.

Despite the staff's ambivalence about her prognosis, Holly faced rehab with true grit. Gripping her walker, Holly inched along the hallway hour after hour, steely determined to achieve full recovery. Word searches and crossword puzzles sharpened her mind. Old family photo albums strengthened her memory.

At times, Holly seemed discouraged, more aware of the hurdles ahead than the incredible obstacles she'd already overcome. But the bounty of encouraging cards and e-mails lifted her spirits. "God's healing me," she told the amazed medical staff, "because so many people are praying!"

After one week of rehab, the staff scheduled a meeting to review the case. By aid of her walker alone, Holly trekked down the long corridor and into the conference room with a broad smile and a great sense of accomplishment. Each doctor and therapist present gave a glowing report of her progress. "The speed of Holly's recovery is nothing short of miraculous!" her rehab physician stated. "Eventually, I expect to see full recovery."

Four weeks after the tragic accident, Holly was discharged! She received word, that very day, of her official acceptance to TEAM as a foreign missionary.

"How soon will I be able to go?" she asked her specialists.

"At best? A year-and-a-half."

She'd survived against all odds and surpassed incredible hurdles. Still, regaining the physical stamina and cognitive ability needed to practice medicine in a remote foreign culture would take time.

At her childhood home, Holly recuperated under her parent's watchful care. Fresh air and sunshine rejuvenated her soul as she rested outside on the patio. Her body had been broken, but nothing could crush Holly's adventurous spirit!

With crutches, a neck brace, and her jaw wired shut, Holly grinned at the bike shop clerk. "They're fixing *me*," she teased, then pointed to her mangled BMX. "Can you fix *this*?" As it was obviously ruined beyond repair, she purchased a new one. Using a device to hold the bicycle stationary, Holly began riding indoors. "I kept threatening to go for a ride outside," she laughed. "But my parents glared at me when I even mentioned it!"

E-mail updates continued. "How thankful I am for your powerful and effective prayers," Holly shared. "I am reminded with a smile of

2 Corinthians 4:7: 'But we have this treasure in jars of clay to show that this all-surpassing power is from God and not from us.' How His power has been evident in my healing so far. Truly, I feel like a 'jar of clay' in His hands. May He mold me into exactly what He wants me to be."

At times, Holly grew weary of the difficult recovery process, but she was grateful to God for sparing her from tragedy. *How did I ever survive?* she wondered after reviewing her medical records. "Without divine intervention," she said, "I would be dead or paralyzed and mentally handicapped. It's hard to be discouraged when I think of that! There are many things to complain about but exceedingly more for which to be thankful."

With many milestones yet to reach on the road to recovery, Holly persevered. Soon, she discarded her crutches, received temporary dentures, and returned to her own apartment. Despite a slight limp, she enjoyed walking up to four miles a day on the shore of Lake Michigan. "It felt great to get outside again!" Gradually, her cognitive skills improved. Gradually, she began feeling like herself once more.

Through attending a conference on family practice medicine with her father, Holly received reassurance that her medical knowledge was "still there." Then, only six months after her brain injury, extensive neurological evaluations confirmed Holly's ability to perform the duties of her occupation. She resumed her medical practice shortly thereafter.

"How grateful I am to be able to work again! I'm certainly more familiar with what it's like to be a patient than I ever cared to be," she laughed, "but I pray this experience will help me become an even better doctor."

Holly was eager to reach the mission field, but lingering injuries required further attention. Numerous surgeries, frequent procedures, and weekly appointments consumed her life for the next twelve months. Although she faced many setbacks and delays in the reconstruction of her jaw and gums, Holly's bright spirit kept shining! "God's just giving me another opportunity to practice patience!" she said. When plagued with pain, Holly used it as a reminder to thank God for her blessings. "Doing so keeps me focused on Him, not my problems."

While restoration of her damaged leg, mouth, and teeth continued,

Holly completed her training with TEAM and prepared for her assignment. She accompanied a mission team on a short-term trip to China, which tested her resilience in a foreign culture. Despite the high altitude (12,000 feet) and twelve-hour time difference—a classic challenge for those who've suffered traumatic brain injury—Holly maintained a steady pace throughout the trip with no fatigue.

Upon returning, Holly traveled to numerous churches and mission conferences to share her testimony of God's healing power. "Truly, we serve a wonderful God who has intervened miraculously. I look over my hospital records, and my medical brain can't quite believe I am well enough, just two years later, to be going to a remote region of Central Asia. Truly, His power has been evident in my healing. The reality of this body being just a 'jar of clay' seems more real to me now!

"Initially, my prognosis was so poor that many people were unsure whether to pray for my healing or pray that God would take me home in peace. In Psalm 50:15 we are told, 'Call upon me in the day of trouble; I will deliver you, and you will honor me.' God surely delivered me from a dramatic life-changing trauma. I pray that every remaining moment of my life will bring Him the honor He deserves."

At last, Holly was released from the care of her physicians. Final preparations were completed, and heart-tugging farewells were exchanged. Filled with the anticipation of a lifetime, Holly boarded the airliner, bound, at last, for her destination. Her destiny.

Before the final flight of her long journey ended, Holly pulled out her Walkman and listened to a new CD. The song she heard echoed the passion in her soul.

> I will go where there are no easy roads,
>   leave the comforts that I know.
> I will go and let this journey be my home.
>   I will go, I will go.
>
> I'll let go of my ambition,
>   cut the roots that run too deep.
> I will learn to give away,
>   what I cannot really keep.

I will go, Lord, where Your glory is unknown;
   I will live for You alone.
I will go because my life is not my own.
   I will go, I will go.[1]

As the jet approached the runway, Holly gazed through the window at her new homeland. Her eyes filled with tears of joy as her heart filled with gratitude to God!

I will not die but live,
   and proclaim what the LORD has done.
      —Psalm 118:17

Lord Jesus, I am rendered utterly speechless by the revelation of Your omnipotence! How awesome are Your mighty works on my behalf! Although the afflictions of the righteous are many, You, O Lord, deliver me from them all. Truly, You are able, by the healing power at work within me, to do abundantly more than all I ask, think, or imagine. To You, O Lord, be the glory, forever and ever! Amen.

PART 3

EXPERIENCE HIS PRESENCE

God Is Ever Present—He Is Always with Me

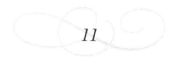

Run to the Cross

TAMMY TRENT

The LORD is close to the brokenhearted
and saves those who are crushed in spirit.

—PSALM 34:18

When I was fifteen, I met an incredible young man in our youth group back home in Grand Rapids, Michigan. Trent and I dated about seven years and married when we were twenty-one and twenty-two. It was the healthiest relationship I've ever known in my life. I'd come from a broken home, so I really never had that kind of security in my life—and Trent was all of that for me.

We had a very healthy marriage. A great marriage. Trent was a man who loved God with all of his heart and spoke that into my life. A man who always believed in me and the things of God for my life. A man who always encouraged me.

We were married for eleven years, and I never heard Trent speak unkind words to me. He never said anything mean or hurtful. Sometimes when I completely deserved it, I'd say, "I just totally chewed you out. Why don't you come back at me? Why don't you just leave?"

"'Cause, Tammy, I never want you to know hurt. I never want you to think that I will ever leave you." That was my life with Trent for eleven years. Always looking for something God had for us around every corner, but together. We completed each other because our love was totally a gift from God.

In September 2001, we went on a mission trip to Jamaica and decided to go a week early to vacation. Trent took me on a great vacation at this all-inclusive resort. We did so many things that week. It's funny when I look back. God was not surprised by any of this. The things He gave me that last week with Trent were just perfect.

On our way to Kingston, Jamaica, for the mission trip, we stopped at a place called the Blue Lagoon. Trent's a scuba diver. He'd been diving since he was twelve and was really good at it. He'd given me a couple of options that day, and I chose this place because I knew it was what he really wanted to do.

There's a hole in the middle of the Blue Lagoon, about 200 feet down. Trent free dives—going without tanks. He can hold his breath up to about five minutes underwater. So we had lunch right there on the dock, then he wanted to explore that hole for about fifteen minutes.

I waited on the dock as Trent waved to me and swam away.

I waited on that dock, overlooking the lagoon, for about thirty minutes. Then forty-five. I started to get concerned cause I didn't see him coming up and down. I knew that to breathe he had to. Feeling a bit of anxiety, I started to cry.

Okay, God. Help me right now, I thought. *I'm okay. I can do this. And he's okay. What do I do God? What do I do?*

Watching for Trent, I saw a boat and asked them to take me out to search for him. We couldn't find anything, but I knew immediately that something was wrong.

I was all alone. I didn't even know where I was.

I called in a dive team. They went down in that hole and searched for Trent for three hours—but found nothing.

"Tammy, we have to call this off and search in the morning." This was Monday evening, September 10.

I woke the next morning, all of my family flying in to be with me. Then the doctor I was staying with took me to the television, showing me the terrorist attack in America. All of my family members were grounded on airplanes. They couldn't reach me at all.

The only person who made it onto the island was Trent's dad. He'd taken the red eye out of Los Angeles and made it in at 8 o'clock that morning, thirty minutes after they told me that they had found Trent.

For two weeks, I couldn't get home, dealing with all of this. But you know what? God had already begun to do something in my life. I'll never forget sitting in the back room of that restaurant on the dock when I knew that something was terribly wrong. I knew this was it. A real test of my faith at that moment of what I would do.

And all I could do was lift my hands saying, "Jesus! Jesus! Help me!" As I sat alone, all I could think of was praise songs. So I started to sing. "I love You, Lord, and I lift my voice. To worship You[1] . . . O, God, fill my life right now!" At that moment, I knew that my life would never be the same.

Doctors were there, and I remember thinking, *I don't care. Tammy, sing! Speak in tongues. If you're filled with the Holy Spirit, just let it flow.*

And I remember finally getting to the hotel and wondering how to go on with life. You see, Trent was everything to me. He was the person that I turned to for everything. Sometimes, when I'd go to God and ask questions, if I didn't have the answers soon enough—I'd go to Trent! "Will you tell me what to do?"

So now I had to learn to trust God. Now I had to really learn.

So I'll never forget one particular day at the hotel. My father and I had adjoining rooms so he could watch out for me, but he was gone the entire day.

Crawling to the bathroom, I sat and cried out to God. "Just send me one angel to hold me. I gotta know all this is real—that You're real. I gotta feel Your presence somehow, cause I'm all alone. Just send me one angel."

I walked out of the bathroom and got myself together. *You can do this, Tammy,* I thought. My bed was all a mess and hearing someone in the adjoining room, I walked in and saw the housekeeper in her full Hilton outfit. So I asked, "Could you come in and just make up my bed for me?"

"Yes. I've been trying to get to you. I could hear you, but I just couldn't get to you," she said. "Can I just come and hold you?"

Oh, I completely fell apart. Tears started to flow as she came in and held me.

"Can I pray with you?" she asked.

Now I had not seen one person since I'd prayed for God to send an angel to hold me. I knew it was God! So we prayed together as she held me.

Then she cleaned my room, just singing songs of praise. I went in the other room and opened the Bible. The first verse I read was Psalm 30:5, "Weeping may endure for a night, but joy comes in the morning" (NKJV). *God, I know I will smile again. I know I will find joy again,* I thought.

Every day since then has been a search for me. Some days people ask how I'm doing, and I don't know how to answer. I feel like I'm learning to breathe again. Putting my life back together again. But I do know, more than anything—*there is hope!* I can stand up and say, *God is real!*

He keeps revealing Himself to me all the time—and in the funniest places.

I was in the sauna the other day at the Y when a woman walked in and started talking about her life. How crazy it is. Working. School. Being a single mom.

"You know what, I'm gonna pray for you."

"Really?" she said.

"Yeah. What's your name? Can I pray for you right now?"

After introducing ourselves, she said, "You know, Tammy, this is so weird. When I saw you walk into the locker room, I knew I was supposed to pray for you. I don't even know you, but I knew it. But I was shy about my faith and couldn't tell you. Then we talk here in the sauna, and now you're going to pray for *me*. Isn't that God!"

We held hands. And we prayed. And we cried. I kept peeking out the window, hoping no one would walk in at that moment. But I thank God for reminding us—one more time—that He cares about us right where we're at.

I don't have all of the answers. I'm still trying to search myself. But I do know this: if you don't have Jesus, you don't have hope.

Just as He's been here for me, He'll be there for you.

The song I share says it so well. It's the very thing I've held on to since thirty minutes after Trent waved good-bye. We have to hang on to it—the Cross where healing waits.

Run to the Cross

When the pain of today
Steals the hope for tomorrow
And you feel like you can't go on
Jesus is waiting
He shares your sorrow
He knows your strength is gone

And He bore the pain that's been breakin' you
So let it go—just let it go

Run to the cross
Leave every care
There in his loving arms
Run to the cross
Where healing waits
Oh the race has been won
For all who will run to the cross.[2]

I will sing of your strength,
   in the morning I will sing of your love;
for you are my fortress,
   my refuge in times of trouble.

—Psalm 59:16

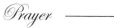

Lord Jesus, You alone are my refuge. When life is more than I can bear, I will run to the Cross and rest in the peace of Your presence. You are my hope, my strength, my ever-present help in times of trouble, heartache, and devastating loss. During the stormy seasons of life, when raging seas crash upon me, my faith will not waver. For in Your presence You hold me firm and secure through every storm. Amen.

A Night of Peril

RICHARD ANDERSON, AS TOLD TO SUE FOSTER

*For he will command his angels concerning you
to guard you in all your ways.*

—PSALM 91:11

Wallets, car keys, jewelry, valuables—now!" Two masked robbers brandished guns at the seven of us huddled in the small storage room in the rear of the recording studio.

"Don't kill us," I pleaded in desperation. "We have families and—"

"Do you think we care about your lives?" the second thug snarled. "A recording studio is soundproof. No one will hear the gun shots."

My heart lurched. *Dear God!* I prayed. *Will we see another day?*

Cursing, the two thugs bound our feet and wrists with layers of duct tape, secured our wrists with electrical chords, and taped our mouths shut.

At gunpoint, I waited my turn. Recalling earlier events of the evening, I tried to make some sense of this horrendous, yet surreal nightmare.

Just a few hours earlier, the six members of our band "Southland" met our sound engineer at a recording studio in Brea, California, to record a CD. We ordered pizza for dinner and were waiting for its arrival. When one of the guys stepped outside to check on our pizza delivery, the armed robbers hurled him back into the room. In shock, I dropped the eight hundred dollar Takamine guitar I was holding.

The two thugs immediately took control, ordering us to line up against the wall.

At least God has provided us with someone trained and equipped to deal with such situations, I thought, glancing at Vance, my police officer friend. *Maybe he has some kind of remote control device he can activate to call for backup.* Searching my friend's face for some sign of reassurance, I was dismayed to behold Vance's ashen, petrified countenance. *Oh, Lord! Vance is as powerless as the rest of us!* I murmured, suddenly feeling weak and lightheaded.

I relived being kicked and beaten as the thugs forcibly herded us from the recording studio into the small rear storage room. An emergency exit door momentarily held a dawning ray of hope. Freedom and the outside world beckoned just beyond. Two fellow band members slammed their massive weight against this door, a vain attempt at making a break for freedom. The establishment had illegally bolted the emergency exit. There was no way of escape. My rising hope was snuffed out like a flickering candle.

Without warning, I was snapped back into the present by a cruel blow to my face. I realized that it was my turn to be tied up. Evidently upset that he had temporarily run out of duct tape, the thug decided to take out his frustration on me. My jaw throbbed from the blow. The electrical cord dug into my flesh as he tied my hands behind my back. The duct tape across my mouth made it difficult to breathe. I felt slightly claustrophobic. *As bad as this is, I know it's just going to get worse,* I thought.

The robbers tied us together in pairs, facing each other, and ordered us to lie down. My partner, Ron, and I toppled over sideways. I found myself facedown on the carpet, unable to see anything. Hurling expletives, the thugs exited the storage room. For a time, our group was left alone, looked in on only occasionally, while the robbers gathered and loaded up our expensive sound equipment.

As I lay with my face pressed against the coarse carpet, I prepared myself to die. I imagined my family's living with the painful memories surrounding my demise. As I reflected on my lost opportunity to experience the growing up of my two preteen sons, I felt a profound sense of sadness. *Never again will Andy, Evan, and I ride bikes together. No more cheering my boys at baseball games. Never again will we play catch in the park. No proud dad to celebrate their high school graduations. Never again to . . .*

My thoughts revolved around speculation as to where the bullet would enter my body and how it would feel to die. *I wonder, will they shoot me in the back or in the head? Will I go fast, or will it be lingering and painful?*

During the intervals when the robbers were preoccupied in the sound room, we prayed quietly. I fervently petitioned the Lord for a miracle. To strengthen and encourage myself, I also recited favorite Scripture verses: "God has said, 'Never will I leave you; never will I forsake you'" (Heb. 13:5). "The Lord says, 'I will rescue those who love me. I will protect those who trust in my name'" (Ps. 91:14 NLT).

Gradually, we assisted each other in pulling the duct tape down below our mouths and were able to communicate in hushed tones.

"Hey, Rich," Ron whispered to me. "Did you feel that strange fanning sensation a few minutes back?"

"Yeah, I sure did, Ron. But it stopped when the robbers left the room."

"You know what, Rich? I think there are angels here with us."

"Yeah, I think so, too. I'm feeling such a powerful presence of God. And an incredible peace." *Never will I leave you; never will I forsake you,* resounded God's promise in my head.

"Me, too!" Ron replied. "I'm not scared in the least."

As the robbers began checking on our group less frequently, we agreed to take action. In hushed tones, Vance urged us, "Listen, you guys. We can't just lie here helplessly on the floor waiting to die. We've got to fight back!"

"You're right, Vance," I responded. "Let's see if we can help each other up and somehow get ourselves untied." Although seemingly impossible, we snapped apart each other's duct tape and electrical chord bindings in mere seconds. Without question, divine intervention was at work.

"All right, guys, this is our chance!" encouraged Vance. "A couple of you charge the rear door. The rest of us grab chairs for self-defense. We'll stand by the door to the sound room. Okay, you guys. At the count of three, go!" Slamming their bodies against the bolted door, just as they had done earlier, two fellow band members miraculously broke it down within the first several attempts.

Now free at last, we scattered and summoned the police. Within minutes, what seemed like the entire police force was on the scene. The robbers had escaped out the front door as soon as they heard the back door crashing down. Although the entire ordeal lasted only forty-five minutes, our interviews with the police at the crime scene continued well into the night. We lost thousands of dollars of equipment as well as personal effects that were never recovered. After months of investigation, the case remains unsolved. I have no regrets about the loss of my possessions, however, for I am exceedingly grateful to God to be alive.

This robbery was, without question, a life-changing event for me. While lying on the floor preparing to die, I realized how fragile life is and how it literally could be over within seconds. But I promised God that if, through some miracle, I made it out alive, my life beginning the very next day would be different because life is too short. I resolved to develop a committed relationship with the Lord and to be God's instrument in touching people's lives through active ministry I would begin to listen to what God was telling me to do.

In looking back on my life following this experience, I am very aware of the hand of God working in remarkable ways. In fact, four years after this horrendous ordeal, I entered the ministry full-time to pastor Capistrano Community Church in San Juan Capistrano, California. I took my promise to the Lord seriously and I've been blessed for it. I believe, without a doubt, that God both protected and delivered us that night!

> Be at rest once more, O my soul,
>   for the LORD has been good to you.
> For you, O LORD, have delivered my soul from death.
>   —Psalm 116:7–8

Almighty God, I worship You from the depths of my heart and exalt Your holy name! For by Your mighty power You protect my life and deliver me from the snare of the wicked. Safe within Your presence, I shall never fear, for truly the angel of the Lord guards all who trust in You, and rescues them from harm. Amen.

13

The Goal

BONNIE TACKETT

The LORD himself goes before you and will be with you;
he will never leave you nor forsake you. Do not be afraid;
do not be discouraged.

−DEUTERONOMY 31:8

The day dawned brightly on that Monday morning. As the alarm clock buzzed on my nightstand, I stretched my arm over to whack it one more time for a few extra minutes of sleep. "Oh-h-h-h," I moaned as my aching body stung my consciousness again. "Okay, Lord, for You. Just for You," I said, trying to focus on my real incentive to get up.

I dressed quickly after showering, grabbed my gear, and went out the door. I had an appointment at the hospital radiology department for a mammogram at 8:15 A.M. I arrived just in time to be told that Registration did not have an order for the test. So, I volunteered to run upstairs to my office, call my doctor to request that a copy be faxed over to me and take it back downstairs to the registration department.

"Typical," I grumbled to myself.

After I received the order, Registration informed me that I had missed my scheduled time of 8:15 A.M. and could be worked in about 1:00 P.M. instead. "All right," I said trying to be polite. One o'clock came, and I headed downstairs for outpatient testing.

After I completed all of the paperwork, a volunteer escorted me to a lovely room that was better furnished than my own living room. I barely had time to sit down on the luxurious sofa before a door opened and the mammography tech asked me to come in. I followed her into another room and then followed her instructions to undress and put on a skimpy gown. I turned to address the cold steel machine in front of me and, feeling valiant, I engaged it almost like engaging the enemy in a war. Stalwartly, I approached and then yielded myself. Arranged and rearranged, I stood there defeated and embarrassed.

Finally, the testing was completed. She noticed on my paperwork that I was an employee at the hospital. She seemingly considered me part of the "family," and went on to show me the developed films.

"I'll have your old films 'couriered' over right away from North Main Imaging for comparison," she said. "If the radiologist wants you to have an ultrasound, we'll call you. What's your extension?"

Couriered over right away? A strange sort of apprehension seized me. This was not the usual procedure when everything was normal. I brought myself back to the situation at hand and numbly said, "4415." She patted me on the back and directed me to get dressed. I fumbled with my clothes, discarded the gown in the dirty laundry bin, and left still in a daze.

I returned to my office and plunged into my work. "Wow, I've been gone over an hour," I muttered to myself. "I'd better hurry up and get going. I'm way behind." The time passed quickly and 6:00 P.M. arrived uneventfully.

"See you guys later. Have a good night," I said to my coworkers as I went out the door. I clocked out and headed for the employee parking garage. As I approached my vehicle, I said my usual, "Thank you, Lord, for my little red car," opened the door, and got in.

All at once, with a fury, the realization of the day's events came to mind. *Hey, Bonnie, this stuff sounds serious,* I said to myself. *You might have breast cancer. You know, the Big C.* My breath disappeared as I was enveloped in a weakness I'd never felt before. Fear flooded my mind and grabbed hold of my heart. I tried to shake it off as I shook my head, turned on the ignition, and drove out of the garage.

My vision suddenly blurred as tears filled my eyes. *Why am I crying? I asked myself. Am I afraid of dying?* No, that wasn't the issue. I'm a Christian and death would be a graduation to glory. "Okay, then, why am I crying?" I asked myself aloud.

Suddenly, the Lord spoke to my heart, reminding me of His truth: "*Perfect love casts out fear*" (1 John 4:18 NASB).

"What am I afraid of, Lord, that I don't realize I'm afraid of?" My son, whom I had not seen or heard from in more than a year came to mind. "Am I afraid that I'll die without seeing him again?" I asked the Lord.

"*Trust in the Lord with all your heart*" (Prov. 3:5).

I acknowledged and answered, "God is sovereign." And then I realized why my appointment time had been rearranged. I began to see His sovereignty in the events of the day. As I mulled over the circumstances, I saw that He had even arranged the timing of my appointment. He knew in advance that I would have had a difficult time trying to cope with the situation all day long in front of my coworkers. The afternoon had flashed by so quickly that I had no time to dwell on myself. He spared me my own self-centered anguish as He kept me busy focusing on others. And He protected me from baring my distracted soul to my unsaved coworkers in a time of weakness. This situation was to be between only the Lord and me.

As I considered my very real physical symptoms that could prove to be those of breast cancer, I prayed, "Lord, help me get through this. I can't do it on my own. You know that and so do I. Do I really have cancer?"

"*Though he slay me, yet will I trust in Him*" (Job 13:15 KJV).

"Lord, I know cancer isn't the issue. Trust is. Help me to trust You more and not just resign myself to a bad situation."

You are more than a conqueror through Him who loves you. (See Romans 8:37.)

"Yes, Lord, not 'survivors,' not 'overcomers' in our own strength, but 'conquerors' through You."

I arrived home; greeted my little Maltese, Frosty, with a big hug; sat down at the computer; and typed out my story. Then, as I anticipated the next day, I went to bed and slept soundly. With peace in my heart and my eyes focused on Jesus, I claimed Philippians 3:12–14: "I press on to take hold of that for which Christ Jesus took hold of me. . . . I do not consider myself yet to have taken hold of it. But one thing I do: Forgetting what is behind and straining toward what is ahead, I press on toward the goal to win the prize for which God has called me heavenward in Christ Jesus."

Regardless of the outcome, Lord Jesus, please help me stand firm and keep on keeping my eyes on You, I prayed.

Two days later. I received a call from my regular doctor. He wanted me to come in. Obediently, I agreed to see him the next day and braced myself for any bad news.

"There's no easy way to say this, Bonnie, so I'll just tell you outright. It looks like you have breast cancer. I want you to see a surgeon right away for a biopsy, and we'll go from there."

Later, when all of the tests were completed and the diagnoses were final, the Lord drenched me in His grace so that I could rest quietly in Him as I underwent chemotherapy, surgery, radiation treatments, and courses of hormone-inhibiting medications. Through it all, He reminded me to look ahead with joyous anticipation to that for which He had called me—the celebration of my victory through Him—the very real ultimate and eternal goal.

Months later, my oncologist informed me that I had a metastatic stage four cancer with a low expectation of a five-year survival time. While there for a follow-up visit, I peeked at his most recent office notes in my medical chart. He stated that there was a real possibility I had been cured.

Excitedly, the words *Praise Jesus* resounded deep within my soul. Confident in Christ and smiling victoriously, I got ready to leave. I went on my way with the words of one of my favorite songs, "Redeemer," ringing true in my mind:

> The very same God that spins things in orbit
> He runs to the weary, the worn and the weak

And the same gentle hands that hold me when I'm broken
They conquered death to bring me victory
Now I know my Redeemer lives, I know my Redeemer lives![1]

"I love You, Lord, and thank You for loving me," I said as I basked in the joy of His presence.

> Praise the LORD.
> How good it is to sing praises to our God,
> how pleasant and fitting to praise him!
> —Psalm 147:1

──────────── *Prayer* ────────────

Lord Jesus, I thank You for being my constant companion and my closest friend! The assurance of your presence gives me great hope. Knowing You are always by my side gives me the strength to face anything that comes my way. I will proclaim Your praise forever and ever! Amen.

14

Sometimes, Solitude Isn't Enough

DORIS E. HACK, AS TOLD TO PACHECO U. PYLE

> *God is our refuge and strength,*
> *an ever-present help in trouble.*
>
> —PSALM 46:1

At five o'clock I shut down the computer. It had been a productive day, catching up on some transcription and actually clearing some files from my desk. I had been working with Youth with a Mission for four years, something of a joke since I was seventy-two. Our office was on the beautiful grounds of Mercy Ships International Training Center in East Texas. I loved my job, but a day at the desk left me pretty drained.

As I left, I called to a coworker, "Bye, Bonnie! See you tomorrow— Lord willing and if the creek don't rise."

It was early February, barely chilly in the daytime but cold once the sun went down. On the rural highways, I passed East Texas pines and pastures, then arrived at an unmarked gate. I drove through onto a fifty-two-acre plot. My house was at the far back corner. Driving the access road across a dam, up a steep hill, and finally down the long driveway to my home, I once again thanked God for the privacy of this place. I love solitude; in fact, I often play solitaire! My only neighbor was a Mercy Ships family who was overseas on an assignment. I had the whole fifty-two acres to myself!

As I got out of the car, I was bone weary, but I made myself take a walk before fixing dinner.

Although the air was mild, I grabbed a jacket, sure that I would need it when the sun went down. Early spring was in the air with a few wild flowers beginning to bloom. As always, I took joy in the beauty of the outdoors.

I retraced some of the way I had just driven—along the driveway to the hill, then down the steep slope and across the dam. While walking along, I was almost euphoric, praising my Father for His love, the beauty around me, the wonderful fragrance of early spring, and especially for His strength to meet this day's needs.

After walking some distance, I turned onto a logging road. Suddenly, without warning, I fell. I don't remember tripping; it was almost as though I had been thrown down. In trying to catch myself, I twisted my body and landed hard on the ground, with excruciating pain in my left leg.

"Oh, Lord! What's happened to my leg?"

I lay quietly for a moment, then tried to get up, but my leg would not support me. I fell back to the ground! The pain was incredible. I lay there, taking stock of the situation. No one would hear me call, but I couldn't spend the night outside when the temperature might fall into the low 30s. I knew I must get back to the house and phone for help. "Oh, Father, show me what to do!"

Near where I lay was a stick about 18 inches long. I reached for it, then removed my jacket and shirt, using the shirt to bind the stick to my leg. I put my jacket back on and tried to stand, only to have the leg buckle again.

Well, I would just crawl! I got up on all fours—well, on "all threes," dragging the fourth—and began the slow trek home, ignoring the pain in my left leg.

Going back to the access road, across the dam, up the steep hill, and down the drive toward the house takes seconds in a car. In my condition, it took two hours.

As I crawled, I was aware of God's presence. Each time I felt like giving up, He would tell me to stop, rest, and take a few deep breaths, but not to lie down.

The palms of my hands were scraped raw, as was the one knee I could use, but I found myself praising Him for being my strength and comfort and wisdom.

The road was unpaved. As I flicked stones aside, I actually chuckled and thanked God for the men who had worked to make the road at least this smooth. And I definitely thanked Him that there were no fire ant mounds in my path, because East Texas is full of them!

By the time I reached my driveway, it was dark and chilly, and I was cold and exhausted. When I saw the light in my kitchen window, all I could say was, "Thank You, Father! Thank You, Jesus!" over and over in a very loud voice!

I pulled myself through the door, newly grateful that my house had no steps. After I phoned some friends who lived a short distance from the acreage, I made it to the refrigerator for some cheese slices.

When my friends arrived, they called 911, then wrapped me up in an afghan and made me some hot tea. They prayed for me, asking especially that just the right doctor would be on hand to attend me.

One of them drove to the highway to flag down the ambulance because we knew the driver might not find the unmarked gate.

The emergency room was brightly lit, and many people were bustling around. After the doctor introduced himself and X rays were taken, someone asked permission to cut off my slacks. By 11 P.M., I was in surgery. Both knobs of the tibia had broken behind the kneecap. The doctor used an external fixator with six pins holding my leg together in a steel arc, looking like something from outer space. There was so much soft tissue damage and internal bleeding that the doctor did a fasciotomy, a six-inch incision on each side of the leg to let blood drain out.

During my eight days in the hospital, I received excellent care. I thanked God that I had access to such medical facilities. In the port cities where Mercy Ships serve, an injury such as mine could not be properly attended.

Word got around the hospital of the seventy-two-year-old woman who clawed (and crawled) her way home in the dark. To my amusement, hospital staff members poked their heads in the door, wanting to see the "tough lady."

Through it all, God's presence was beyond words. I realized that He was not only *with* me but also *in* me in a way that I had never known. He was Christ in me, the hope of glory. Not I, but Christ was living His life in me—which made the leg His leg as well as mine, and His responsibility!

Soon, my daughter Pat arrived from California to help. With the assistance of a friend, they got me into the car and home.

My cat, Li'l Darlin', ignored me for days, probably offended that I had been gone so long. Finally, one day he jumped onto my bed and stayed close from then on.

Pat, a family practice physician's assistant, gave me expert care for ten days. Then Mary, my daughter from the Chicago area, came to take care of me for a week. Despite the circumstances, I had wonderful mom-daughter times with each of them.

Of course, I missed my independence. One night, Li'l Darlin' wanted out. I could have called Mary but was sure I could do it myself. Wrong.

Somehow, I caught my walker on the edge of the carpet and fell backward, striking both my head and the fixator on the floor. Amazingly, my head and my leg were okay, but my pride was hurt, and Mary wasn't at all happy with me.

Annie, a friend for some forty years, was my next caregiver. She came from Indiana and stayed two-and-a-half weeks. Because of an infection at the site of one of the pins, I took a round of antibiotics and was very weak. I would say to Annie, "I think I'll take a walk around the block." Then I would lean on my walker and go carefully around the living room couch.

Christine, a special friend as well as my boss at work, was next. She moved in with me, along with her husband and nine-year-old daughter. They have been a great help and comfort.

Throughout this time, my friends assured me of their love. I realize now that no matter how precious solitude is, there are times when the presence of others is absolutely essential!

After about nine weeks of physical therapy, I was dismissed with no promise I would ever fully recover the use of my leg.

Now, I'm 76 years old, and my Father has been gracious indeed. Instead of an isolated house in Texas, I now live in Daytona Beach, Florida, in a tenth-floor condo. Most of the time, I use the elevator, but on occasion, I've taken the stairs just because I can! I work for Christian Adventures International and walk up the stairs to my second-floor office. My badly injured leg works just fine, and I thank the Lord!

Did I feel God's presence through my entire ordeal? No, but I can't live by feelings. The Bible tells me that He will never leave me, never forsake me. The pain of that experience in Texas is part of the "all things" that work together for good for my welfare.

Solitude seems a thing of the past, but I'm not complaining. I've found out the hard way that sometimes solitude just isn't enough.

> I know the LORD is always with me.
>   I will not be shaken for he is right beside me.
> No wonder my heart is filled with joy,
>   and my mouth shouts his praises!
> —Psalm 16:8–9 NLT

Prayer

Lord God, I thank You for the gift of Your presence that dwells within me. With You as my steadfast companion, I am never truly alone. I praise You for the continual presence of the Holy Spirit who comforts and strengthens me when I am weak. Cleanse me, dear Jesus, whenever sin creeps in and clutters my heart, blocking my awareness of Your holy presence. Amen.

15

The Everlasting Arms

LOIS PECCE

The eternal God is thy refuge,
and underneath are the everlasting arms.

—DEUTERONOMY 33:27 KJV

After enduring hours of hard, unsuccessful labor, our daughter Linda was rushed into surgery for an emergency cesarean section. As her labor coach, I was allowed to "suit up" in disposable scrubs and sit in a corner of the operating room. I watched anxiously while the physician worked, then held my breath as he scooped a tiny ball of humanity into his hands and passed her to the waiting nurse.

At the far side of the room, the nurses busied themselves with the baby. I heard a brief cry of protest at being suctioned followed by long minutes of silence. *Is she okay?* I worried. At last, the nurse carried her to her mother and I saw that little Lindsey's eyes were wide open, exploring her surroundings. I realized at once that here was a child too eager to be about the business of discovery to waste time crying.

She looked so beautiful, so perfect that when they told us a few hours later that she had major heart abnormalities I had trouble believing it. The ambulance crew wheeled her travel isolette to Lind bedside before taking Lindsey away to Children's Hospital Medical Center in Cincinnati. I videotaped the baby contentedly grasping her mother's finger, her eyes seeking in the direction of her mother's voice. I also captured the sad little wail when they took her from the room and wheeled her down the hall. It was as if she *knew.*

My heart wanted to run after her, hold her, and comfort her. I felt torn between the needs of my daughter, the needs of my grandchild, and the demands of my employment.

Although still in considerable pain, Linda was relieved when they released her two days post-op. "We're going to Cincinnati," she said. I didn't argue. She endured the winter-rough roads and heavy traffic without complaint; her only thought was getting to her baby.

At the hospital, her own pain again became lost in the pain of watching them draw blood samples from her child. "I can't look, Mom!"

Lindsey had already learned that when someone touched her heel, it was probably going to hurt. It amazed me how strongly this seven-pounder could kick! Wishing that they could take my blood instead of hers, I cradled and comforted her while I held her foot so they could take the necessary samples. *If only it was me going under the knife and not this helpless baby,* I pleaded silently, even as I thanked God that the miracles of modern medicine would give her a chance to live.

The day before surgery, as I yearned again to trade places, the thought came to me: *You cannot trade your blood or your life, no matter how much you love this child. But this is exactly what Jesus did for you. Only the King of heaven could come to earth to trade places—to trade His life-blood and His life for yours, and for everyone He created!*

One week after Lindsey's birth, our whole family gathered anxiously in the waiting room as the surgeons prepared to operate. They'd already told us that one in every one hundred live births in the United `ates has some form of heart defect. Lindsey was the one in eight `nd live births to have transposition of the great vessels of the `rse positions of the aorta and pulmonary artery) along with `tween the lower heart chambers. In the old days, she `alled a "blue baby" because of insufficient oxygen `y to cut and reposition the major vessels and to `ith Dacron would take at least eight to nine hours.

The nurse assistant came through the doors during the second hour. "They've laid open her chest and the surgeon is reviewing his strategy before he operates. Lindsey made a good transition to the heart-lung machine. She's on a 'cold table,' which markedly slows her heart rate and should help to prevent brain damage from lack of oxygen or seizures."

I'd prayed before, constantly for months, for the safe arrival of this grandchild, but as I thought of the risks and pictured her tiny form lying on that terribly cold table surrounded by lights, people, and equipment, my heart cried out to God again.

As quickly as the one picture came to mind, there came another, as clear as though I could see it. Beneath the child, cushioning her against the harsh cold, were the loving hands of God, cradling and supporting her. Words from Deuteronomy 33:27 came to memory: "The eternal God is your refuge, and underneath are the everlasting arms."

Fear left me. I knew that whether Lindsey lived or died, she was safely in God's hands. Thankfully, she lived. This bright, inquisitive, deeply loving child is a joy in our lives.

Later, after Lindsey came home from almost a full month in the hospital, I wrote to several prison inmates with whom I corresponded, telling them of the waiting room experience.

When one young man read the story, God placed a special vision in his mind. A week or so later, I received a large envelope from the prison. Inside, I found a lovely colored-pencil drawing that he'd created on the back of a large poster, which he'd carefully folded in half.

On one side, he'd drawn the compassionate face of God as He reached down through the clouds with an outstretched hand. In His palm lay a swaddled infant, sleeping peacefully. All about Him, angels dressed in rainbow colors came and went to do His bidding.

I turned the folded sheet over and read the title, "'The Surgeon,' because God is the surgeon in all of our lives!" In his fanciest printing, he wrote the text of Deuteronomy 33:27.

What a treasure! Tears came to my eyes as I held this visual depiction of God's everlasting arms. Tears of gratitude for His comfort to us and healing of our grandchild. Tears of thankfulness that God's arms are never too short to reach us wherever we are, even in prison.

Years later, our granddaughter asked about the scars on her chest. We told her about the surgery and explained about the picture that hangs in her room. "Who is the baby?" she wanted to know. "Was that me?"

"Yes, that was you. But it is also each person who especially needs God's care." We try to help her understand that no matter what, when, or where we are, God is watching over us, loving us, and caring for us—holding each of us in His "everlasting arms."

I sought the LORD, and he answered me;
 he delivered me from all my fears.
Those who look to him are radiant;
 their faces are never covered with shame.
—Psalm 34:4–5

Prayer

Lord, I cannot say why one much-loved child should live and another die. These things are beyond our knowing and understanding. This world is full of brokenness that cannot be fully healed until You come again and make things new. But this I do know: Your love is everlasting and Your compassions are "new every morning" (Lam. 3:23). You delight in innocence and bringing joy to human hearts. I praise You every day for Your goodness. Amen.

PART 4

EXPERIENCE HIS MERCY

God Gives Even When We Don't Deserve It

16

Turning Point

Michael W. Smith

" . . . when you seek me with all your heart.
I will be found by you," declares the Lord, *"and will bring*
you back from captivity."

–JEREMIAH 29:13-14

When I was in high school, I played piano, but I lived for baseball. I envisioned myself someday in front of cheering crowds, holding a bat, not a microphone. Then, when I was fifteen, I didn't make the all-star team. My dream was suddenly crushed. I had no idea that the closing of that door would open another that was far beyond what I could have possibly imagined.

I had become a Christian when I was ten and was active in our family's church, but my involvement increased when my baseball career ended. Every Sunday night, I played piano for our praise gatherings. Our youth choir performed incredible musicals, which featured music that was very different from the hymns we sang on Sunday morning. I started listening to artists from the Jesus movement of the early 1970s, and I liked what I heard. I "delighted" in the music and the friendships that I found in my youth group. Only looking back years later do I see that God was planting the seeds of desire so that I would grow into my career in music.

Just as Christ told a parable about young plants choked out by weeds, my story could have had a similar ending. As you're about to discover, my journey involved a detour that could have destroyed all that I now cherish. Perhaps you can learn from my mistakes.

After growing up in a loving Christian home, giving my heart to Christ as a boy, and being involved in a great church, I hit the skids my junior year of high school. Some of my closest friends graduated and moved off to college or got married. Without that circle of support, I started hanging out with people who offered me everything I had managed to avoid up to that point. I was testing limits, taking chances, and acting crazy.

When I moved to Nashville in 1978, I sank deeper into that lifestyle. Because I was no longer under the protective eyes of my small-town family and friends, I responded to my newfound freedom with more habits that enslaved me. I kept late hours and wouldn't wake up until afternoon. I was experimenting with drugs and trying to impress people with how cool I was. Instead of acknowledging my musical abilities as a precious gift from God, I took them for granted.

With each step deeper into the mire, I grew more unhappy, more depressed. One night after we had played at a bar, everybody in the band went over to one guy's house to party. There I made a near-fatal error by trying a drug that caused an extremely violent reaction. On the way home, I thought I was losing my mind. I stayed up all night, terrified about what had happened. I remember praying over and over, "God, don't let me die." The next day, I began to recover from the ordeal, but I still didn't take the very large hint to run from that lifestyle.

During a visit to my parents' home, I remember vividly having a quiet but uncomfortable conversation with my father on the porch. With knowing eyes, he softly said, "You're going to have to straighten out your life." He knew that I didn't need a lecture. His few words communicated both the hurt and the love that he felt. Although I knew that my dad was right, I didn't have the faith and self-control to turn from the dead-end alley I was traveling.

In October 1979, I had an experience that I would describe as similar to a minor nervous breakdown. Psalm 38:4–6 paints a pretty accurate picture of what was going on inside me:

> For my iniquities have gone over my head;
> Like a heavy burden they are too heavy for me.
> My wounds are foul and festering
> Because of my foolishness.
> I am troubled, I am bowed down greatly;
> I go mourning all the day long. (NKJV)

The day I hit bottom I was alone in the house. I began to freak out. My thoughts raced. My heart pounded. My body shook. For hours, I lay on the kitchen floor, curled up like a baby.

I can't explain all that was going on inside me, but there came a specific moment when I felt that God joined me there on the floor. He didn't come to condemn me or reprimand me. I already knew that my life was totally out of control. Instead, He came to lift the burden that was crushing me, and to free me to start again. Inside I knew that God was saying, *This is your turning point.* The next day, I could sense that my life was taking a new direction.

Although things have not been all blue skies and rainbows since those reckless years, I've come to recognize that God's ways are far better than mine. Just as my life turned from self-destruction, God started to give me glimpses of what lay in store if I would just delight myself in Him:

> For I know the thoughts that I think toward you, says the LORD, thoughts of peace and not of evil, to give you a future and a hope. Then you will call upon Me and go and pray to Me, and I will listen to you. And you will seek Me and find Me, when you search for Me with all your heart. I will be found by you, says the LORD, and I will bring you back from your captivity. (Jeremiah 29:11–14 NKJV)

The Lord really did bring me back from being captive—from being cool and acting in total rebellion—to doing what I knew to be right.

Don't deceive yourself by thinking that you are too strong or too smart to stumble. At fifteen, I would have said there was no way I would ever place myself in some of the situations that grew far too familiar. Sin will take you farther, keep you longer, and cost you more than you can ever see at the outset.

If you are being held captive, Christ offers the key to your freedom. He said, "Whoever commits sin is a slave of sin. And a slave does not abide in the house forever, but a son abides forever. Therefore if the Son makes you free, you shall be free indeed" (John 8:34–36 NKJV).

Not only will the Son make you free but also His Father has promised to give you a future and a hope.

In my anguish I cried out to the LORD,
and he answered by setting me free.
—Psalm 118:5

Father God, in humility and adoration I worship You! From the depths of my soul, I praise You, Lord Jesus, for the freedom I've found in You! By Your mighty power and outstretched arm, You set me free from the grip of destruction. No soul is beyond Your reach, no captive beyond the rescue of Your omnipotent hand. For nothing is impossible with You! Amen.

17

Affair Repair

NANCY C. ANDERSON

And Jesus said unto her, Neither do I condemn thee:
go, and sin no more.

—JOHN 8:11 KJV

If anyone ever tells you, "I didn't plan to have an affair—it just happened," they're not telling the truth. We all make choices—and our choices have natural consequences. The Bible asks, "Can a man take fire to his bosom, and his clothes not be burned?" (Prov. 6:27 NKJV). I literally flirted with disaster and brought an inferno into my heart and home.

Ron was twenty-six, and I was twenty-two when we got married in 1978. Both of us believed that it was the other person's job to "make me happy." We soon found out—that was impossible! I complained and criticized my way through our first year, and then Ron retaliated with the "I'm-a-bad-husband-because-you're-a-bad-wife" defense. Our anger and resentment grew until it overshadowed our love.

That's when I met Jake. He thought I was beautiful, funny, and smart. He only saw the good in me and bathed me in compliments. We worked for the same company, so it was easy to spend time together. We started meeting for lunches, then dinners, and eventually dessert.

I have no excuses; I knew exactly what I was doing. I chose to enjoy his lingering gaze, I chose to return his flirtations, and I chose to welcome his kiss. I chose to have an affair.

In June 1980, I told my husband what he already knew: "Our marriage is falling apart; we're both miserable." Then I surprised him with, "So, I need some time to think—I'm moving out." (I didn't tell him about Jake.)

He begged me to stay. "I won't yell at you anymore—I'll be a better husband—please don't go." I ignored his pleas and moved into a motel.

Jake and I started making secret plans for our future. He was married and had two children, but he was going to leave them—for me.

I had purposefully kept my Christian parents in the dark about our marriage problems, and because they lived in a different state, that tactic worked—for a while.

One day, as I was visiting our condo, packing some more of my things, my mother called. She asked. "Honey, are you all right?"

"Sure, Mom, I'm fine," I lied.

"I don't think you are. I think you're in some sort of trouble because last night I woke up several times and felt compelled to pray for you. I want you to talk to your father—he's on the other line."

I am in trouble now, I thought. *I've never been able to lie to my father.* "Hi, Daddy," I whispered.

"Hello, honey, your mother is convinced that you are in need of her midnight prayers. Are you?"

I hesitated, took a deep breath and said, "Yes."

"Tell us everything."

I said, "I've moved out of the house, and I'm going to file for divorce."

Then, after he heard what I wanted to do, my father said a prayer that changed everything. He prayed that I would consider the consequences of my actions and that I would stop—before it was too late. He asked the Lord to draw me to His side, lead me back into His light, and give me the strength to follow His will instead of my own.

After I hung up the phone, I made another call—to God. I had been avoiding Him for months. My guilt, shame, and sin had built a wall between us. However, I broke through the wall as I surrendered my will and my heart and asked the Lord for the strength to make a full confession to Ron. When I told Ron about Jake and asked for his forgiveness, he miraculously chose to forgive me.

Then we both talked to Jake. He was stunned when Ron and I told him that we were going to stay married. I cried as I apologized to Jake and explained why I had to quit my job and the reasons I could never see him again. Ron and I asked him not to call or have further contact, and he agreed to honor our request. I told him that I hoped he would reconcile with his wife and restore his family. When we said good-bye, all three of us were crying—for three different reasons.

My feelings for Jake had not changed. I was still "in love" with him, but I chose to stay with my husband. It was out of obedience at first, but as I began to act lovingly, the loving feelings eventually followed. Ron and I began to rebuild our marriage with Jesus as our new foundation and God's Word as our new floor plan. We planted a sturdy hedge of protection (safeguards) around the perimeter. Ron and I are living proof that no marriage is beyond repair.

I played with fire, foolishly thinking that I would not be burned, but my self-centered choices charred my whole family and Jake's, too. Each lie I told and each sin that I committed affected others. I don't know if Jake and his family were reunited, but I pray that they were.

Ron and I recently celebrated our twenty-fifth wedding anniversary, and I am thrilled to tell you that we are deeply and tenderly in love—with each other!

> Praise be to the Lord,
>   for he has heard my cry for mercy.
> The Lord is my strength and my shield;
>   my heart trusts in him, and I am helped.
>   —Psalm 28:6–7

Prayer

Father of all mercy, humbly I bow before Your throne. I thank You that when I confess my sin You are faithful and just to forgive, cleanse, and purify me of all unrighteousness. I am forever grateful for the grace and mercy I've received through my Lord, Jesus Christ. With Your comfort and strength, draw near to all who have experienced the unbearable pain of betrayal. By the power of the Holy Spirit, heal every broken heart and restore every broken relationship. Amen.

The Piano

PACHECO U. PYLE

He who conceals his sins does not prosper,
but whoever confesses and renounces them finds mercy.

—PROVERBS 28:13

Our family has moved again, and the piano has made the trip reasonably well with only a broken caster. I touch the top of the aged upright, and I remember.

When I was a child, I sat at this keyboard, as had my older sisters before me. Often, I would get Grandma Umphress to tell me about the time the house caught fire and the piano was saved only because someone shoved it out a window.

The fire occurred about 1906, and the piano had been in the family more than ten years by that time. Grandma had played it, and my father, his brother, and his sisters had taken lessons at its keyboard. When my father was a boy, he hated piano lessons so much that he tried to avoid them by begging to work in the cotton fields on their farm outside Dallas, Texas.

But the best story connected with my 1895 Wheelock piano involved the day Mitchell Arphaxad (Phax) Umphress, my grandfather, bought the instrument.

It was the day before Christmas, and he had taken three wagons loaded with bales of cotton to Dallas to sell. The trip yielded him a good roll of cash. In true Christmas spirit, he bought a box of oranges, a box of apples, a stalk of bananas, a jug of whiskey, and gifts for the family. But his grandest purchase was the piano for his oldest daughter to "give lessons on."

After loading the purchases on one wagon, he sent the other wagons home and stopped in a saloon near the marketplace. A big man, Grandpa was expected to play Santa Claus at the community church that night, but he was sure he had time for a drink in celebration of his good cotton crop.

Grandpa was a heavy drinker, and his involvement in saloon brawls was frequent and intense. Once he gouged out a man's left eye, leaving him permanently blinded on that side!

That day, Grandpa soon drank himself into a stupor. His son-in-law came into the saloon and tried to get him to go home, but Grandpa refused.

The next thing he knew, he woke up in the back room of the saloon, his money gone. Stumbling outside, he found that it was late at night and his mules and wagon were gone. So were the family gifts and the piano. All he had left was a .45 revolver.

He made his way down the street to a lumber company and crawled in between two stacks of lumber. Those wagonloads of cotton represented his year's work. The family expected gifts and money for their winter needs. And he found himself wondering if the children had had a Santa Claus at their Christmas Eve service.

Feeling utterly humiliated and disgraced, he remembered his occasional struggles to quit liquor. They had always ended in failure.

"Lord, forgive me," he prayed. "I'm a complete failure. I might as well get out of the way and stop being an embarrassment to my family."

Taking the revolver, he placed the barrel into his mouth. But just as he was ready to pull the trigger, the thought came: *Liquor did this to me. I'll just go home and face the whole thing. I'll never drink again.*

But he felt so bad; his head ached with a hangover. How could he possibly face his family at a time like this without a drink?

He went back into the saloon. "Sam," he said, "I'm going to quit. Give me a half pint to taper off on, and I'll pay you the next time I'm here."

The saloon owner looked at his customer closely. "You really mean it, Phax?"

"Yes, Sam. I do." Grandpa told Sam what had happened.

Sam knew Grandpa and liked him. He said, "Well, if you're going to quit, you're not going to get any whiskey in here. And you can't buy it anywhere else 'cause they won't sell it to you on credit. You just take your hat in your hand and go on home."

The distance home was about ten miles, and Grandpa's courage must have wavered many times during the walk.

As he neared his house, he saw the mules that had been hitched to the wagonload of gifts. They were quietly grazing in the pasture. He wondered how they had gotten home.

Approaching the house, he heard shouts of Christmas morning gaiety. And then, amazed, he heard the sound of a piano!

He hurried across the yard and onto the front porch. Bursting into the house, he found his large family laughing over their gifts and admiring the tones of the big piano.

When Grandpa's son-in-law had been unable to get him to leave the saloon, he had taken his money and had driven the wagon home. Quietly, he told the family that Grandpa was drunk and would be home later. The son-in-law, a big man himself, donned the Santa outfit and took over at the church celebration. No one was the wiser, except the family, and they already knew Grandpa's weakness.

But Grandpa remembered his crisis. He had faced death between those stacks of lumber, and his resolve was now genuine. As he put it, "God brought me out, and I was going to quit drinking if it killed me."

For a year and a half, he stayed at home, refusing to go anywhere that sold liquor. After that time, he finally went to town and was greeted by his old friends.

"Phax, where've you been? Come on and let's have a drink."
He always refused. He never drank again.

God allowed my grandfather to come to death, but even then, He prepared an answer that would mean new life. My piano reminds me of His great mercy.

> Praise be to the God and Father of our Lord Jesus Christ! In his
> great mercy he has given us new birth into a living hope.
>
> —1 Peter 1:3

Prayer

Lord Jesus, with a humble heart I confess my sin and thank You for the mercy and forgiveness You grant to me. I praise You Lord, for empowering me with the strength to break free from every addiction and unhealthy habit that threatens to destroy my life and harm my loved ones. With gratitude, I proclaim the mercy and faithfulness You have shown to me! Amen.

19

Changing a Life

LEE STROBEL

Let us come boldly to the throne of grace, that we may receive
mercy and find grace to help us in our times of need.

—HEBREWS 4:16 WNT

After a trip to Atlanta for an interview with author William Lane Craig, I got into my rental car and took a leisurely drive up Interstate 75 to Rome, Georgia. The next morning was cool but sunny, and I got dressed and headed over to a church for Sunday services.

Outside, politely greeting everyone with a handshake as they arrived, was William Neal Moore, looking handsome in a tan suit with dark stripes, a crisp white shirt, and brown tie. His face was deep mahogany, his black hair was close-cropped, but what I remember most was his smile. It was at once shy and warm, gentle and sincere, winsome and loving. It made me feel welcome.

"Praise the Lord, Brother Moore!" declared an elderly woman as she grasped his hand briefly and then shuffled inside.

Moore is an ordained minister at the church, which is sandwiched between two housing projects in the racially mixed community. He is a doting father, a devoted husband, a faithful provider, a hard-working employee, and a man of compassion and prayer who spends his spare time helping hurting people whom everyone else seems to have forgotten. In short, he's a model citizen.

But turn back the calendar to May 1984. At that time, Moore was locked in the death-watch cell at the Georgia State Penitentiary, down the hallway from the electric chair, where his life was scheduled to be snuffed out in less than seventy-two hours.

This was not the case of an innocent man's being railroaded by the justice system. Unquestionably, Moore was a murderer. He had admitted as much. After a childhood of poverty and occasional petty crimes, he had joined the Army and later became depressed by marital and financial woes. One night he got drunk and broke into the house of seventy-seven-year-old Fredger Stapleton, who was known to keep large amounts of cash in his bedroom.

From behind a door, Stapleton let loose with a shotgun blast, and Moore fired back with a pistol. Stapleton was killed instantly, and within minutes Moore was fleeing with $5,600. An informant tipped police, and the next morning Moore was arrested at his trailer outside of town.

Caught with the proceeds from the crime, Moore admitted his guilt and was sentenced to death. He had squandered his life and turned to violence, and now he himself would face a violent end.

But the William Neal Moore who was counting down the hours to his scheduled execution was not the same person who had murdered Fredger Stapleton. Shortly after being imprisoned, two church leaders visited Moore at the request of his mother. They told him about the mercy and hope that was available through Jesus Christ.

"Nobody had ever told me that Jesus loves me and died for me," Moore explained during my visit to Georgia. "It was a love I could feel. It was a love I wanted. It was a love I *needed*."

On that day, Moore said yes to Christ's free gift of forgiveness and eternal life, and he was promptly baptized in a small tub that was used by prison trustees. He would never be the same.

For sixteen years on Death Row, Moore was like a missionary among the other inmates. He led Bible studies and conducted prayer sessions. He counseled prisoners and introduced many of them to faith in Jesus Christ. Some churches actually sent people to Death Row to be counseled by him. He took dozens of Bible courses by correspondence. He won the forgiveness of his victim's family. He became known as "The Peacemaker" because his cellblock, largely populated by inmates who had become Christians through his influence, was always the safest, the quietest, and the most orderly cellblock in the prison.

Meanwhile, Moore inched closer and closer to execution. Legally speaking, his case was a hopeless cause. Since he had pleaded guilty, there were virtually no legal issues that might win his release on appeal. Time after time, the courts reaffirmed his death sentence.

So profound was the depth of Moore's transformation, however, that people began to take notice. Mother Teresa and others started campaigning to save his life. "Billy's not what he was then," said a former inmate who had met Moore in prison. "If you kill him today, you're killing a body, but a body with a different mind. It would be like executing the wrong man."

Praising him for not only being rehabilitated but also being "an agent of the rehabilitation of others," an editorial in *The Atlanta Journal-Constitution* declared: "In the eyes of many, he is a saintly figure."[1]

Just hours before Moore was scheduled to be strapped into the electric chair, shortly before his head and right calf were to be shaved so that the lethal electrodes could be attached, the courts surprised nearly everyone by issuing a temporary stay to his execution.

Even more amazingly, the Georgia Board of Pardons and Parole later voted unanimously to spare his life by commuting his sentence to life in prison. But what was *really* astounding—in fact, unprecedented in modern Georgia history—was when the Parole and Pardon Board decided that Moore, an admitted and once-condemned armed robber and murderer, should go free. On November 8, 1991, he was released.

As I sat with Moore in his home overlooking a landscape of lush pine trees, I asked him about the source of his amazing metamorphosis.

"It was the prison rehabilitation system that did it, right?" I asked.

Moore laughed. "No, it wasn't that," he replied.

"Then it was a self-help program or having a positive mental attitude," I suggested.

He shook his head emphatically. "No, not that, either."

"Prozac? Transcendental meditation? Psychological counseling?"

"Come on, Lee," he said. "You know it wasn't any of those."

He was right. I knew the real reason. I just wanted to hear him say it. "Then what was responsible for the transformation of Billy Moore?" I asked.

"Plain and simple, it was Jesus Christ," he declared adamantly. "He changed me in ways I could never have changed on my own. He gave me a reason to live. He helped me do the right thing. He gave me a heart for others. He saved my soul."

That's the power of faith to change a human life. "Therefore," wrote the apostle Paul, "if anyone is in Christ, he is a new creation; the old has gone, the new has come!" (2 Cor. 5:17).

Billy Moore the Christian is not the same as Billy Moore the killer. God had intervened with His forgiveness, with His mercy, with His power, and with the abiding presence of His Spirit. That same kind of transforming grace is available to everyone who acts on the ample evidence for Jesus Christ by deciding to turn away from their sin and embrace Him as their forgiver and leader.

It's awaiting all those who say yes to God and His ways.

Praise be to the LORD,
    for he has heard my cry for mercy.
The LORD is my strength and my shield;
    my heart trusts in him, and I am helped.
                    —Psalm 28:6–7

Lord Jesus, in utter humility and gratitude I fall before Your throne. Thank You for the precious blood You shed to cover all of my sin. Your forgiveness is beyond measure! Because Your mercy is infinite, You do not deal with me as my sins deserve. How I praise You for Your willingness to change the lives of those who respond to the Truth and open their hearts to You. May Your tremendous love be a healing balm to every soul that has been a victim of violence. Amen.

PART 5

EXPERIENCE HIS SOVEREIGNTY

We Believe God and Obey What He Says

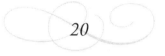

The Gift

LINDA EVANS SHEPHERD

Those who hope in the LORD
will renew their strength.
They will soar on wings like eagles;
they will run and not grow weary,
they will walk and not be faint.

—ISAIAH 40:31

I sat in the stillness of my twenty-month-old daughter's hospital room, holding her hand, watching for signs of life. As I studied her, Laura looked as if her dark lashes would flutter open and she would sit up, ending our almost two-month-long nightmare. How I longed to hear Laura's giggle as she snuggled with her silky hair against my cheek while I read to her from one of her favorite books.

Impulsively, I leaned over and kissed her cherubic face. "Honey, it's Mommy. I love you. I know you're in there. I'm waiting." The words caught in my throat. I shut my eyes. If only I could turn back the hands of time and avoid the collision that had saturated our lives with grief.

I remembered sitting in the emergency waiting room with my husband, tearfully waiting for the doctor's verdict. Paul and I hugged each other and shouted with joy when the doctor told us, "Laura's going to be all right; go home and get some rest." But as I lay my head on my pillow, my dreams spun out of control. I awoke in a cold sweat, picturing the blood that had trickled out of Laura's ear. *Laura is not okay. The crash was too violent. I have to get back to the hospital!*

I raced through the rain-slick, predawn streets. Once in Laura's ICU room, I found the staff gathered around her body as it quaked with convulsions.

God, where are You? I cried like David, the psalmist.

Three months later, Laura had been moved to another hospital, yet she remained unresponsive. I continued to cry, *Lord, when will You answer our prayers?*

One evening as I sat by her bed, the mechanical breathing of her respirator jarred my thoughts. A strange mood of uncertainty settled over me. I looked at the child I had fought and prayed so hard to keep. *She's really in there, isn't she?* I stood up, trying to shake the doubt that had suddenly caught me off guard. Noticing that my watch read 11:00 P.M., I began to get ready for bed. Paul was still out of town, so I had decided to sleep there in Laura's room.

The nurses had already completed their evening rounds, so I flipped off the lights and shut the door. It would be hours before anyone would check on us. I felt alone, too alone. I popped two extra-strength pain relievers and set the bottle on a nearby tray table beside my glass of water. *What if the doctors are right and Laura never wakes up?* I thought as I spread a blanket in the window seat. Fluffing my pillow, I wondered about God. *Maybe He's abandoned us. Maybe He isn't going to answer my prayers.*

This new thought punctured my tired spirit. *Just who am I trying to fool?* I questioned. *I need to face facts. Laura will never awaken. She'll live the rest of her life as a vegetable, hooked to life support.*

I tried to stifle the emotions that began to boil as Laura's respirator mocked, "no-hope, no-hope, no-hope." My chest constricted as I gasped for air. Everything seemed so different, so pointless. Laura, I decided, would be better off dead than in some suspended state of life. How could we allow our precious daughter to live out her days in that condition?

A plan rose from my grief. I couldn't bear to ask the doctors to take my child off life support after I had already prevented this action once before. But now, I realized that Laura's smile would never return. My dreams for her life were dashed. And God? He had been as silent as Laura's stilled voice.

I was truly alone—miles from my husband, miles from Laura's cognizance, and light years from the God I had trusted. Perhaps God's silence meant that I needed to take matters into my own hands. Perhaps it was up to me to end her horrible suffering.

I can kill Laura without the doctor's help, I reasoned. *I can turn off the alarms and unplug the vent from the wall. It would be so simple, except,* I wondered, *if I kill my daughter, how can I live with myself? How can I face Paul or my parents?*

The moonlight reflected on my bottle of painkillers. If I swallowed them, no one would find us until morning. Laura and I could escape this living hell together.

Just as my plan seemed like the only solution, I found my hand resting on my belly. My hidden child was only two weeks old, but I knew he was there.

My thoughts slowly cleared. *How can I kill myself? How can I kill Laura? A new life is growing inside me. A life that has the right to live!*

As my reasoning returned, I whispered a prayer. "Lord, I'm willing to wait on You, no matter the pain and the cost." The word *wait* jolted Isaiah 40:31 into my consciousness: "They that wait upon the LORD shall renew their strength; they shall mount up with wings as eagles; they shall run, and not be weary; and they shall walk, and not faint" (KJV).

I cried myself to sleep, terrified of the future, terrified of the murders I had almost committed.

Nine months later, my daughter began to emerge from her coma just before her baby brother, Jimmy, was born.

Although her eyes fluttered open, her gaze was fixed. She remained hooked to life support, and she slumped in her wheelchair, totally paralyzed. We were told that Laura was blind, but she began to greet us with a cheerful, "Hi!" And slowly, her eyes began to focus once again.

Although I still sometimes weep over the Laura I have lost, I embrace the Laura who has returned. How glad I am that I waited on God instead of going through with my murderous midnight plan. I still face obstacles, but God enables me to run the race set before me—a race that I now know I can finish.

The Lord is my strength and my shield;
my heart trusts in him, and I am helped.
—Psalm 28:7

Father God, You alone are the strength of my heart and my life! Although pain and sorrow envelop me, I will trust in Your sovereign wisdom. Lord, I surrender all of my cares to You. When I am weary, uphold me with Your mighty arm and help me to walk in victory. My body and my mind might become weak, but the Lord is my strength. He is mine forever! Amen.

21

A Commuter Marriage

CHUCK NOON AND MARITA LITTAUER

Trust in the LORD *with all your heart*
and lean not on your own understanding;
in all your ways acknowledge him,
and he will make your paths straight.

—PROVERBS 3:5-6

The nature of crisis is that when it is yours, it is huge. You can logically measure your problem with someone else's and realize that you do not have it so bad, but that lasts only so long. As soon as your situation hits you in the face, you are overwhelmed again. For months, Chuck and Marita wrestled in their spirit over their crisis.

Three years ago, because of some upheaval in Chuck's industry as a counselor, he was forced to seek new employment. When he couldn't find anything locally, he began to look out of state and found a job in Colorado, five-and-a-half hours away from their New Mexico home. The problem was that Marita didn't want to move out of state. "I have an established business with great employees and a creative job I enjoy. We have good friends and a strong church here."

While they'd moved several times before for his job, Marita told

Chuck that she wasn't moving this time. She didn't want him to take the job so far away.

But then one day Chuck came home and told her that he'd accepted the position. His unilateral decision angered Marita, who began to make his life "very unpleasant." "We had several long, tearful, heated 'discussions,'" she said.

Chuck was surprised by Marita's response. "Marita has followed me in several moves. While I always had a job, I couldn't quite get ahead. So when the economy turned downward and I lost my position, I was crushed. I tried to pursue employment locally but just wasn't able to find anything in my field. Believing that better opportunities awaited me as a counselor in Colorado, I became licensed there and was able to find a job."

"When I told Marita, she was upset," Chuck continued. "I couldn't understand why she wouldn't want to move if it meant my success. After all, she'd moved before. I felt she needed to support me."

Marita felt differently. "Why does everything have to be about *his* job? Doesn't he realize how important my business and having security is? Plus, if this new job doesn't work out, what will we do? My business has been supporting us during Chuck's unemployment."

Marita spent a lot of time praying about it, and one day during her devotions she wondered what God would want for her life. "It doesn't take a theologian to figure out God's priority," Marita said. "Should I put my business first or my marriage first? If I believe in the Bible, I know I have to put my marriage first, which, in this case, meant accepting a move. If God gave me this business, which I believe He did, He'll take care of it."

So she told Chuck they'd move. "The amazing thing," Marita said, "is that the moment I reached this decision, when I chose to put my marriage first and submit to my husband's needs, my sense of crisis lifted, and I was at peace with the situation."

Chuck and Marita found an apartment to rent in Colorado and decided for the time being that Chuck would live there during the week while Marita stayed at their home. She'd drive to Colorado on weekends. Marita got him settled into his new pad, decorated it, cooked him some meals to keep in the freezer, and returned to their home in New Mexico until she'd be able to make the move permanently.

Chuck was thrilled with their decision. He enjoyed his job and thought that everything was going well. Marita drove back and forth between Albuquerque and Colorado Springs almost every weekend. But the stress and exhaustion of their commuter marriage was taking a toll. Marita had three automobile accidents.

One evening six months into their arrangement, Chuck was outside walking his dog, Harley, when he felt God speak clearly to him. "I heard God tell me, 'Go home and take care of your wife,'" Chuck said. "This wasn't what I wanted to hear!" He struggled with what God told him. Chuck thought, *If I do what God's asking, I really ought to be in the same state as my wife.* But he didn't want to leave his job. He knew he wouldn't find anything back in New Mexico—which meant he'd have to give up his field of study, everything he'd trained for. "I just didn't want to do that," Chuck admitted. "I saw great strides happening in my clients." But God's words kept coming back to him.

Chuck didn't tell Marita about his encounter with God. So when he quit his job in Colorado and moved back to New Mexico, she was shocked.

"I assumed when I submitted to what God had told me about making the move," Marita said, "it would be permanent. So when Chuck moved back here, I couldn't believe it!"

Chuck took a job that he considered beneath his abilities and education and ended up working there for a year and a half. During that time, God began to work with Chuck in a way He hadn't been able to before. "I was so caught up with the success of my career that I began to put God and my wife in the background," Chuck said. While working at this job, he read the Bible through cover-to-cover. And he didn't try to look for a better position. "I felt as if God wanted to teach me something that I couldn't learn if I was working in my field," Chuck said. "Once I put my wife, not my career or my search for success, first, I was offered a job in my field that was impressive and paid more than I'd ever made." Since that time, Chuck's been offered many other positions and has had his pick of opportunities.

"When I was seeking success and my own interests," Chuck said, "success eluded me. When I was willing to do what was best for my marriage, I found the success I had worked so hard to find. Ecclesiastes

9:9 says, 'Live happily with the woman you love through the fleeting days of life, for the wife God gives you is your best reward down here for all your earthly toil' (TLB). Those words have been true for me."

Marita agreed. "That period of our life was difficult," she said. "But God used it to teach us about the true meaning of sacrifice and loving each other and God extravagantly. Although God's way doesn't seem to make sense to the world, it is the best. And I do know that God is in control!"

I will come and proclaim your mighty acts, O Sovereign LORD; I will proclaim your righteousness, yours alone. Since my youth, O God, you have taught me, and to this day I declare your marvelous deeds.

—Psalm 71:16–17

 Prayer

Lord God, I praise Your holy name for Your ways are always best! Your wisdom is infinite, and I trust You to guide me in all of my endeavors. When life is uncertain, I will rest assured that You are always in control. When circumstances cause fear or anxiety, gently remind me that my life is secure in Your sovereign hands. Amen.

22

Living for the Dream

BRYANT L. HEFLIN

"For I know the plans I have for you," declares the LORD,
"plans to prosper you and not to harm you, plans to give you
a hope and a future."

−JEREMIAH 29:11

The score is tied at 67. Thirty-two seconds remain in the all-star contest at the University of Kentucky. At the horn, both teams break huddle and hustle onto the hardwood. Spectators watch in silent anticipation. The visitors take possession and dribble to midcourt. Sweat glistening on his forehead, Tim Combs steals the ball. He charges toward the hoop as the crowd cheers wildly. Dodging opponents left and right, Tim drives past the defense. He leaps. He shoots. He scores—clinching the final basket and victory for the home team! Proud fans erupt into applause at the brilliant climax of UK's summer basketball camp.

"Great game, Tim! Keep up the hard work." The coach looks the athlete square in the eye. "You've got real potential, son. Potential to go all the way."

It was a moment thirteen-year-old Tim would never forget—the moment his dream was born!

Determined to make his dream of playing Division-I college basketball a reality, Tim accepted the challenge. He pursued the game with a passion. Everything else was a distant second.

Each day after school, Tim practiced in his driveway, perfecting lay-ups, free throws, and dribbling skills until well after dark.

"Hey son," his father often called from the front door. "Ready to come in for dinner?"

"Not yet, Pop," Tim said, catching his breath.

Mr. Combs shook his head and smiled. He and his son had shared a love for the game ever since he'd taken the boy to a "pass, dribble, and shoot" contest years earlier. Tim came home with a toothless grin—and the first place trophy! Admiring his two older brothers, the little sport proudly placed his first award on the shelf with their athletic trophies.

At thirteen, six-foot-one Tim towered over his peers. "At this rate, Mrs. Combs," the family doctor stated, "he'll be six-six, six-seven, before he stops growing." The gears of Tim's mind spun into motion. *Cha-ching!* Visions of a six-figure income swirled in his head. Wide-eyed Tim dared to imagine being drafted one day by the NBA.

As basketball season approached, the agile eighth-grader pushed himself to the max. Recognizing Tim's raw potential, Coach Helsinger encouraged him to strive even harder.

Practice and perseverance soon paid off. Tim earned a starting position on the junior high team. His size, strength, and sharp reflexes gave him a natural edge on the court. Cruising to the hoop, the "go-to" dynamo was unstoppable, averaging twenty points per game.

Each week he led the Indians to victory, as his proud parents cheered him on from the stands. Tim soon gained the admiration of friends and spectators alike.

"This kid's gonna be somethin' when he gets to varsity," opposing team coaches told his parents. But the easy-going teen never boasted. As a Christian, Tim knew that his athletic ability was a gift from God.

With a 15-1 record, the Indians concluded the season as league tournament champs! Basketball gave Tim what all teens crave—an identity. A chance to excel.

Driven by his dream, Tim trained with intensity year round. He ran track each spring and cross-country in the fall. Summer basketball camp fortified his skills and fueled his goal of playing one day for his favorite team, the University of Kentucky Wildcats.

Despite his parents' offer of a Christian education, Tim moved on to Carlisle High School. His success in athletics attracted the attention of the school's other coaches.

"With your speed, we'd love to see you come out for football," said one.

"Look forward to seeing you on varsity, Tim," the head basketball coach assured.

So Tim practiced relentlessly. No arctic blast or drifted snow could cool his intensity. Unable to feel his glove-layered hands, Tim pounded the basketball against the pavement for hours each day. Spurred by raw hunger to reach his personal best, it never seemed like work.

Lifting a book, however, proved to be more challenging. Although he was a bright student, Tim seldom applied his full potential. But staying eligible to compete year round forced him to earn good grades. He performed well in his favorite classes, but academics could never hold his interest like basketball.

Over time, even his relationship with God shifted into low gear. Tim had prayed to receive Christ at the age of six but leaned more on his parent's faith than his own. Sure, he attended church and youth activities, but racing down the road of life, Tim never allowed Christ to take the wheel. His faith was sort of packed away like a forgotten treasure, retrieved only when around church friends and family to maintain the status quo.

Focused on his goal, Tim held on as starter and leading scorer for Carlisle's freshman and junior varsity teams consecutively. While his predicted growth spurt remained on standby, his teammates gained altitude and speed. With duplicate 18–2 records, the team stole back-to-back tournament championships!

By age sixteen, Tim relished the taste of triumph. With a winning record and fans comparing him to former high school hoop stars playing for the NCAA, he was motivated to keep believing in his dream. Without a doubt, Tim knew that basketball was his ticket to success!

After years of training, the junior was pumped with anticipation as he advanced to the varsity squad. He poured all of his energy into preseason practice sessions, eager to earn a starting position.

But days before the season opener, Tim came down with a brutal bout of the flu. While wrestling with the ill-timed virus, he missed several practices before Carlisle's contest against archrival Springboro High. Although eager for his long-awaited varsity debut, Tim watched the battle from the bench, disappointment crushing the driven athlete.

Game by game, an unexplainable pattern emerged. The ace saw limited action and received few opportunities to help his team win. During one game, Coach Johnson* sent him in for the second period. Unleashing his full potential, Tim burst into action, scoring ten points within minutes. But abruptly, a solitary turnover benched the fireball for the rest of the game. Any hope of affecting Carlisle's varsity that season soon perished.

Tim kept quiet, never questioning authority, never lashing out, but unresolved confusion fueled the turmoil in his soul. Trouble escalated when teammates and assistants urged Coach Johnson to play him. In disbelief, Tim walked through his worst nightmare—one game at a time. He prayed for a breakthrough, but halfway through the rocky season came one final blow.

Shouting. Laughter. Slamming lockers. Towels tossed on the floor. Tim grabbed his duffel bag and ambled with his buddies out the locker-room door.

"See you a minute, Tim?" a voice called from a nearby office.

"Hey, Coach!" He stepped into the room. "What's up?"

The assistant coach motioned Tim to close the door. The teen sank into a chair.

"I know it's been rough," he said, fidgeting with a pencil. "I hate to tell you. Starting tomorrow, you're going down to JV." He dropped his gaze. "Sorry, Sport. Coach gave no explanation."

Tim's eyes glazed with shock. Nausea seized his gut as he choked back his anger.

Wanting to crawl in a hole and die, Tim showed up for JV practice

---

* Pseudonym.

every afternoon. Humiliation trailed the teen like a stalker through the halls of Carlisle High. Every glance felt like a laser beam branding him "failure." Pushing his body into the cold wind, Tim raced home every evening, emotion bottled up inside. *Why is this happening? All my hard work and effort for this?*

Tim watched helplessly—hopelessly—as his dream was torn from his grasp. Tossing and turning, he lay awake for hours, night after night. Sleep offered no escape as nightmares invaded his slumber. Tim's parents ached with compassion but found it impossible to console their hurting son. His pain was too deep for human touch. It was a pain that only God's hand could reach, a wound that only God's salve could heal.

Agony and brokenness drove Tim to his knees. Turning to Jesus, he poured out his anxiety. Focusing his undivided attention on God improved Tim's "I" sight. Like putting on new eyeglasses, Tim could clearly see that his priorities were way off track. After years of seeking significance through athletics, basketball was more than Tim's identity. Basketball had become his idol.

This revelation hit Tim hard and fast. Humbled, he buried his face in his hands. "Oh God, how foolish I've been to elevate my talent and my ambitions above You," he pleaded. "You alone deserve first place in my life. Help me change my ways!"

Every morning before school, Tim spent time alone with God in the locker-room, a solitary place where he could pray, study the Bible, and read a daily devotional. The light of God's truth exposed the futility of his self-centered dream. *This is vain,* he thought. *So what if I play in the NBA and rake in big bucks. It's all vain!*

Consistent prayer and Bible study became Tim's top priority. His spiritual growth skyrocketed as God's Word came alive. He identified with the story of Joseph in Genesis 50 and began to see what others "intended for harm . . . God intended for good." By divine sovereignty, God allowed this trial for a purpose.

"Okay, God," Tim prayed, surrendering his shattered dream. "I know You're in control. I'm going to trust You even though I don't understand."

"Tim," a close friend advised, "you can either get bitter or get better and move on with your life."

Tim accepted the challenge. Determined to live for God's dream, he pursued the Lord with all of his heart. Everything else was a distant second.

"Mom? Dad?" he said one evening at dinner. "I know I turned down your offer before . . ."

Mrs. Combs shot a surprised glance at her husband.

"But, after praying about it," he said, "for senior year, I want to go to Dayton Christian High School."

God thrust Tim into Dayton Christian Schools. Little did he know that this turning point was a key to his future.

Tim's senior year at Dayton Christian was phenomenal—a balance of sports, academics, and spiritual development.

Competing for the Crusaders, Tim ran cross-country, his team capturing the single-A state championship. He went out for track, placing third statewide in the 800-meter. Wearing Crusader purple and gold, Tim returned to the game he loved and played with intensity for the glory of God. After a successful season, the senior was selected for Greater Dayton second-team all-area.

Upon graduation, Tim received an academic scholarship and an opportunity to play basketball for Bryan College, a small Christian school in Tennessee. Although it was not the Division-I team he once dreamed of playing for, Tim was elated.

The freshman worked diligently in the classroom and on the court. But between academics and basketball, Tim found college life a tough balancing act. As he endured the demanding schedule, pressure to perform mounted.

Despite his intensity for the Lions, Tim saw little court time during actual games. Shorter and slower than several talented players ahead of him, he began to recognize the writing on the wall. At the end of his first college season, Tim hung up his basketball jersey for the last time. Ready to embrace God's plan, Tim released his grip on the final tattered remnant of his dream and poured his energy into coursework and college ministries.

No longer seeking success through athletics, Tim found his identity and satisfaction as a child of God. *Maybe I don't have fame or fortune,* he reasoned, *but I have a real relationship with the Living God!*

A spiritual greenhouse, Bryan College provided the perfect environment for Tim to grow in the wisdom and grace of God. The city boy cultivated a love for this slow-paced farming community and considered an occupation in agriculture for a time, but God was preparing Tim for another kind of harvest. *I don't want you to plant seeds in the ground; I want you to plant seeds in kid's hearts.*

At times, his thoughts drifted, his soul still ached. *What if I'd arrogantly followed my dream? Gotten a full ride to play ball at a major university?* Then, snapping to his senses, he struck down any bitterness. *God knows what's best for me! He loved me enough to break me of my idolatry! Without Him, I'm nothing.*

In 1990, Tim graduated from Bryan College with a degree in Biblical Studies and committed his career—and his life—to serving the Lord.

Following God's plan, the grad received a master's degree in education and returned to Dayton Christian Schools, serving as a teacher, coach, counselor, and principal. A God-fearing man of integrity and humility, Tim earned the respect of faculty, parents, and students, as well as the admiration of a lovely young teacher, who became his wife.

Living for the dream, Tim maintains intensity, eyes focused on his goal: to reach kids for the glory of God. Connecting with students comes naturally for the firm, yet fun-loving teacher. Because he believes that teaching is more a mission than an occupation, Tim hangs out in the lunchroom and shows up at sporting events to lend moral support, eyes watchful of students needing encouragement. Listening with his heart, he knows when to be tender and when to be tough.

In the classroom, Tim teaches academics and valuable life lessons in light of God's Truth. With creative visuals, he challenges students to be their best for God.

A spring breeze from an open window cooled the third-floor classroom. Except for two rowdy boys in the back row, all eyes were riveted on the history teacher, Mr. Combs. Speaking to his seventh graders, Tim stopped abruptly. While striding toward the back, he reached into his pocket, pulled out his wallet, and—threw it out the window! With mouths gaping and eyes wide open, the students stared as the teacher walked back.

"You know, wasting time in class is as foolish as throwing my wallet out the window! I've got money. Credit cards. Valuable stuff in there," his gaze piercing each student. "You know, I didn't care about school. Wasted my time. But I found out that didn't get me anywhere. I don't want you to end up like that. It's not worth it!"

"Now, Nate," he said with a grin, "run downstairs and get my wallet!"

Goal-driven as ever, Tim's aim is set high. *Am I glorifying God with my life? Affecting those in my sphere of influence for eternity?* His image may never appear on a box of breakfast cereal, but Tim will always be a champion in the hearts of his students—a trophy of God's grace. "Well done, good and faithful servant" is the only accolade he desires to hear ringing in his ears. Faithfully following the Lord, Tim knows that living for God's dream is the only ticket to success!

The Sovereign LORD helps me, I will not be dismayed. Therefore, I have set my face like a stone, determined to do his will. And I know that I will triumph.

—Isaiah 50:7 NLT

Prayer

Lord Jesus, You alone are worthy of all honor, glory, and praise! With reverence and humility, I worship You, for Your wisdom and sovereignty are perfect. I surrender all of my plans, goals, desires, and dreams to You. Lord God, You alone know the purposes that are right and best for me. Even when circumstances are beyond my understanding, I will trust Your mighty hand to guide my life! Amen.

23

The Hearing

BONNIE TACKETT

*And we know that in all things God works for
the good of those who love him, who have been called
according to his purpose.*

−ROMANS 8:28

A whisper of a prayer slipped from my mouth as I stepped out of the elevator on my way to the hospital garage and my parked car. A sense of desperation mounted in my heart and my peace seemingly evaporated as I anticipated another denial by the Bureau of Workman's Compensation. Today marked the last possible appeal. I had tentatively decided that a lawsuit against my previous employer, although "looming on the horizon" as put forth by my lawyer, did not bring me solace but instead brought me an aching uneasiness.

"Lord, please help me," I begged. "I know that You are sovereign over all things, and work through our authorities. I'm asking just this once if I could win this one. You know the truth, and You know me. And please, Lord, if it doesn't go my way, give me the grace to accept it, knowing that You'll provide for me somehow. I'll thank You for whatever You're going to do."

As I drove along the highway en route to the hearing, the familiar music and lyrics of the song "Redeemer" by Nicole Coleman-Mullen replayed in my head. I had listened to her CD several times just before leaving my office at the hospital to calm myself and get my thoughts refocused on things of the Lord.

> Who taught the sun where to stand in the morning?
> Who told the ocean you can only come this far?
> Who told the moon where to hide 'til evening?
> Whose words alone can catch a falling star?[1]

After all, He is in charge, I told myself. *Trust in the Lord with all your heart. If He is for me, who can be against me?*

I pulled into the parking lot of the building housing the "Bureau." I walked inside halfheartedly and took the elevator up to the third floor waiting room and the hearing conference room. My eyes panned the large room, searching for my lawyer. Not a trace of him. I pulled out my notice of the hearing to double check the date and time.

Yup, it's today, and it's 2:00 p.m., I reassured myself as I spotted the clock on the wall.

Oh, Lord, where is Don?

I found a place to sit right in front of the entrance, hoping that he wouldn't have to trip over me to get past. I waited. No lawyer.

Suddenly, a well-dressed older man came up to me and cautiously asked if I was Ms. Tackett.

Just as cautiously, I replied, "Well, yes, but—"

He said, "I'm Jack Cee* with Alex & Darwin.* Don couldn't make it, and he asked me to sit in on this one for you."

"Oh," I said. I tried to regain my composure as my hopes of answered prayer disintegrated.

"I've been doing Worker's Comp cases for thirty-six years," he said. "You see, I really do read the cases and especially the medical documentation by the doctors."

I looked at him with crinkled eyebrows and squinting eyes as I

---

* Pseudonym.

thought, *You're supposed to do that. That's nothing new. That's what you get paid to do.* Rather than express my rising displeasure and condescension, however, I simply answered, "Uh-h-h, okay."

Someone official-looking announced my name and that of my previous employer and directed us to Conference Room 1. As Jack and I walked to the room, he opened a legal-sized folder, scanned its contents, and kept one of his fingers inside, holding his place on some documented notes.

Once inside the room, the Hearing Officer, this time a woman, asked if the employer's attorney was out in the waiting room. Jack said, "I saw him talking to somebody, but he didn't appear to be here for this hearing."

The Hearing Officer did not seem pleased. This was the second time that no one from the other side showed up for the hearing. She asked Jack if he wanted to make any comments or new remarks about the case.

"Yes, indeed I do," he said. With that, he went on to point out that my carpal tunnel problem, after being surgically repaired in the right hand, had greatly improved within two weeks following the procedure. "And," he added, "if her diabetes was the cause of the problem, her hand would not have gotten better."

Wow! I thought. *That's right! This guy is sharp! I never even thought about that, and yet there it was right in front of me all the time!*

And Don never mentioned it—not to me and not to the previous Hearing Officer. He had never said anything noteworthy like that. He had just repeated the same phrase over and over again: "Repetitive typing. Just repetitive typing," as he shrugged his shoulders and shook his head.

Stunned at what I had heard from this man, I almost gloated to myself. As the Hearing Officer proceeded to ask me for the dates of time off, quitting my job, and being hired at my current position, I saw the corners of Jack's mouth just slightly curl into a smile.

"I will make my ruling shortly, and you will be notified of my decision via the U.S. mail. That's all for today."

Jack and I rose from our seats and left the room. As we walked, he placed his hand on my shoulder and said reassuringly, "I think we got it. When she asked for the dates, she was thinking about TTD."

"What is TTD?"

"Temporary Total Disability."

"Really? Really?" I asked excitedly.

"Oh, yes," he replied.

I placed my hand on his shoulder this time and said, "You're sharp. You're g-o-o-d. You really are good!"

"I just read the doctor's notes," he said shrugging his shoulders. "You gotta read the notes."

There it was. God had orchestrated the whole thing right in front of my eyes. He had moved people around like chess pieces on a board and had arranged events in time so that Jack would be at my hearing while Don was busy somewhere else.

"Lord, forgive me for my bad attitude, my condescension, and my thinking the situation hopeless. Forgive me for my lack of faith and forgetting who You are and how You provide for me. Thank You, Jesus, for giving Jack experience, wisdom, and enlightenment. Thank You, Lord."

I returned to work that afternoon with a growing sense of excited joy. I knew in my heart that something good was to come from all of this.

The hearing occurred on Wednesday, and that night passed quickly. Thursday passed especially quickly as I became quite busy at the office. Friday, on returning home, I decided to check my mailbox and see what bills had arrived for the month. I opened the little door, peeked inside, grabbed the contents, and continued on my way. After entering my apartment, I glanced at the mail. There, lying where I had thrown it, amid the bills and ads, was an envelope from the Bureau of Worker's Compensation. I snatched it, tore it open, and there it was!

"It is the finding of the Hearing Officer that the claimant contracted an occupational disease in the course of and arising out of employment. It is therefore ordered that this claim be allowed for: BILATERAL CARPAL TUNNEL SYNDROME." The Record of Proceedings went on to order disability compensation for later periods concerning time off to have the left hand repaired.

As I continued to read, I cheered, "Y-e-e-e-s-s-s! Thank You, Jesus. Thank You, Jesus. I love *You*, Lord. I really do!"

The Lord's provision thrilled me and humbled my heart. I saw again the work of my Redeemer.

I will be joyful in the God of my salvation. The Sovereign LORD is my strength! He will make me as surefooted as a deer and bring me safely over the mountains.

—Habakkuk 3:18–19 NLT

Prayer

Father God, You are sovereign! Your thoughts are higher than my thoughts; Your ways are higher than my ways. In the midst of my uncertain circumstances, You orchestrate all things for my good and ultimately for Your kingdom purposes. Lord, please help me to remember that You are always in control. Those who trust in You will never be put to shame. Amen.

24

One of Us Is Gonna Get It

ROBERT K. LEMASTER

He who dwells in the shelter of the Most High
will rest in the shadow of the Almighty.
—PSALM 91:1

Meaningless! Meaningless! . . . Utterly meaningless!
Everything is meaningless.
—ECCLESIASTES 1:2

The strength in his hands. I'll never forget the strength in his hands. As I helped Dad out of the bathtub, the power of his grip took me by complete surprise. He grabbed my wrists and held on so tightly. I can remember, even now, the softness of his palms. How strange, the calluses earned from over sixty years of exhausting physical labor had completely disappeared.

"One of us is gonna get it!" he pronounced in his strong, matter-of-fact voice. He looked me in the eye, our noses almost touching through the steamy air created by the hot water. His face dripped from the shower as I dried his body; my face dripped from the sweat of the just-completed battle. The last battle. A week later, my dad was gone.

One of us is gonna get it. Nonsensical words at the time. After all, I'm a nurse by profession. I'd bathed the victims of Alzheimer's disease many times before. I easily recognized the wild look in his eyes, the fear that comes from not knowing who you are, or where you are, or who this uninvited stranger is, coolly helping with your most intimate needs.

As we looked at each other through the water dripping from each of our foreheads, I felt as if I were looking in a mirror. You see, I inherited my dad's physical appearance: short and stocky, thick arms and strong back, and nearly identical facial features. I've always enjoyed looking at old photos of his teenage years, proud to hear the words, "You look just like your dad!"

He spent forty-one years acquiring those strong hands by working in a hot, dirty factory so that his three children could earn college educations, an opportunity he never had. He never called in sick. You see, he wanted us to receive a better wage than he could ever earn. He wanted us to work in clean, quiet, air-conditioned offices, in crisp white shirts and the power ties of the executive world, instead of grimy coveralls and well-worn boots. I think of these things as I feel the softness of my clean, smooth hands. No calluses. I gaze in the mirror at my spotless white uniform. *One of us is gonna get it.*

Prostate cancer is a terrible disease, especially when it shows itself late. After the diseased cells have infiltrated the bone and the brain. After the X rays show bones that look like honeycombs, and the once-strong body is emaciated and racked with pain. It seems as if we were in the doctor's office just days after the retirement party, even though these two events were separated by a few undisturbed years.

Unbelievable joy, intense pain. Couldn't he have had just a little more time in between? Before hearing words like *radical prostatectomy* and *radiation therapy?* Before the sickening pronouncement, "We didn't get it all?" Before the suffocating reality of living life centered on doctor's appointments, blood draws, and prescription refills?

One of us is gonna get it. But my dad? Why him? Why now?

> There is a time for everything, and a season for every activity under heaven.
>
> —Ecclesiastes 3:1

The provision of God is truly comforting to experience, truly amazing to watch. Inner strength rises to the surface when least expected. The love of a wife of forty-five years, almost half a century. Sitting next to her husband's recliner in the back room, she held his hand so tightly, showing not a hint of willingness to ever let go, as she reoriented him to a life that was slowly slipping away. To love and to honor, in sickness and in health, 'til death do us part.

Children and grandchildren gathered at his feet, encouraging remembrances from childhood and adolescence. Fascinated by the skill of the storyteller, we laughed at the joy of his telling the story of another successful prank pulled on a brother, a neighbor, a schoolteacher, or a friend. *How can he remember such long-ago details when he doesn't even remember my name?* My own precious wife held her father-in-law's hand, patting it gently. She rehearsed some often-used phrase known by us all, that, when repeated as we walked into the room, brought a smile or an outburst of laughter. While Dad slept, all of us gathered, discussing the next week's work schedules, or planning trips to the lab, or the pharmacy, or the grocery.

Integrity. The character of a man has been devalued in today's world. Honesty, discipline, faithfulness, forgiveness, compassion, love—attributes that have significance only when lived out in the flesh-and-blood reality of family and relationships. Words that strike a powerful chord when spoken, producing a longing for intimacy and security, but, when personally encountered in the course of daily routine, these traits encouraged and inspired all of those who were blessed by his touch.

Dad died on Easter Sunday, surrounded by his family, in the home where he raised us. We all recognized his passing, as the last breath escaped his worn, weakened body. I knelt close, stethoscope in place, listening for one last beat from a heart that had given so much to each of us. The hospice nurse arrived shortly afterward, making the necessary phone calls and arrangements that always attend death. We shared final hugs and reassuring words of peace.

Then I helped the funeral director as we gently lifted the clay shell that once hosted my dad's powerful soul, onto the cart. This precious body, pampered by each of us as we cared for his physical needs near the end, now entrusted to a stranger. Dad's body was leaving home for the last time, but at that very moment, his soul was returning home to his Creator. We all knew that God would heal Dad, and now that healing was taking place as Dad stood face-to-face with Jesus in heaven. How he must have enjoyed feeling the strength in his newly perfected body! How he must have wept upon recognizing his Lord's face through tear-filled eyes, welcoming him to his forever home! *One of us is gonna get it.*

> Now all has been heard; here is the conclusion of the matter: Fear God and keep his commandments, for this is the whole duty of man.
> —Ecclesiastes 12:13

There were so many details—final details. Shopping for a new tie for Dad to wear—his last tie. It took me back to the day, more than a decade past, when Dad asked me to help him pick out a new suit—dark gray, with a hint of a pinstripe. We spent the day together—talking, laughing, and enjoying being together. We purchased new shirts, new shoes, a new belt, and two new ties. "You pick 'em out," he said. He was always known as sharply dressed. Now he trusted my judgment. He always looked great in that suit.

I learned something about Dad at the funeral. The preacher who had known him since his new birth in Christ recalled the day Dad became saved. He was so excited he didn't go to work the next day. You see, Dad needed to spend the day with his wife and family. He needed to visit some friends and make a few phone calls to family members, two hundred miles away—people who had been praying for his redemption. He needed to tell them that he had committed his life to Jesus. But Dad didn't call in sick when he told his boss he wouldn't be at work that day—he said he was calling in "saved."

And Mom's final request. She asked me to ensure that the funeral director removed Dad's eyeglasses before the casket was closed. He had been instructed, but I assured Mom that I would speak with him. After everyone had gone, I watched from the back of the room as Dad's glasses were gently removed. A wave of grief swept over me as I realized that we had completed our call to lovingly care for Dad's body until the very end. Then something unexpected—a device gently lowered Dad's body deep into the casket, and I wept as I watched him disappear, forever.

But no, not really forever, just for a little while. For as surely as our bodies are lowered, they are raised again to eternity, the true reality of life. I know the next time my eyes meet Dad's, he will know my name, and he will recognize my face. And we will have an eternity to worship our Lord together, to fellowship with family and friends. But for now, I dry my tears with my Dad's own handkerchief, the very one I watched him use so many times before to wipe the sweat from his brow, the tears from his eyes, or the dirt from a little boy's hands—my hands. I remember, and I know. *Both of us got it, Dad. Both of us got it.*

> And I heard a loud voice from the throne saying, "Now the dwelling of God is with men, and he will live with them. They will be his people, and God himself will be with them and be their God. He will wipe every tear from their eyes. There will be no more death or crying or pain."
>
> —Revelation 21:3–4

As Easter approaches again, the first Resurrection Sunday I will celebrate without my dad, the memories of the last year are still fresh, still painful. They still bring grief and mourning. But the hope of a future Easter is real, and I know that someday I will celebrate our Lord's ultimate sacrifice, His ultimate gift, in heaven together with my earthly father and my heavenly Father.

Make no mistake—death is real. But eternal life is just as much a reality, and God is my hope for my own resurrection day!

> May the God of hope fill you with all joy and peace as you trust in him, so that you may overflow with hope by the power of the Holy Spirit.
>
> —Romans 15:13

Heavenly Father, You are the one, true source of hope in every season of life. Clinging to the hope I find in You saturates my soul with peace and enables me to cope with pain and loss. By Your grace, I do not grieve as those who have no hope. I proclaim Your praise for demonstrating Your Father's heart to me through Your Son, Jesus Christ, and for His gift of eternal life! Amen.

IN MEMORY OF
HERBERT LEMASTER JR.
1931–2000

Vessels

LORI Z. SCOTT

For we are God's masterpiece. He has created us anew
in Christ Jesus, so that we can do the good things he
planned for us long ago.

—EPHESIANS 2:10 NLT

I remember the day when the intangible feeling of invincibility disappeared from my life as abruptly as a slap in the face. I was a college freshman, and it was my birthday, March 16, 1984, when the doctor announced that I had diabetes.

The diagnosis burst my bubble of general complacency toward infirmity. I tortured myself by reading statistics about the effects of possible complications that accompany diabetes, such as blindness, kidney failure, and neuropathy.

Treatment seemed an unending tightrope of tedious balance with overeating a slow suicide and under eating an unacceptable risk. Questions consumed my mind. *Why me? How will my life be affected? How could I look so normal on the outside while inside I wasted away? I felt too young to face my frailty.*

My parents provided support, but their kindness held a worrisome edge seen in those trying to hide disappointment or fear. I suppose that dealing with a child suddenly afflicted with an incurable disease does that to people. Nevertheless, they loved me and somehow understood that I needed to find my own answers to the questions that plagued me. They encouraged me to seek answers in the Bible.

Pouring through the pages, I found little consolation until I came across a passage in Romans. One verse stood out, though I can't explain why, for it didn't sound particularly comforting: "Does not the potter have the right to make out of the same lump of clay some pottery for noble purposes and some for common use?" (Rom. 9:21).

Contemplating the verse in light of my expectations for the future, I concluded that I wasn't a vessel for noble purposes. How could I be with an illness that infested every aspect of my life like an invasive spider web? I was flawed and therefore a pot of common use, made that way by the Potter Himself.

Assuming that God couldn't use me to make an impact for Him because of my diabetes, I swallowed, resigned. Yet hope remained like a forgotten ember, for my childhood Sunday School teachings stayed stubbornly with me. Three strongholds couldn't be shaken. My thoughts are not God's thoughts. He loves me. I can trust Him. Thus reassured, I eventually adjusted to the special precautions I had to take and returned to a joyful, if cautious, state of mind.

Years later, when I became an elementary school teacher, I discovered how God could use my diabetes to touch lives in a way that wouldn't have been possible without the disease.

My role was instructor and mom-away-from-home. I provided children with learning, encouragement, compassion, and acceptance. They returned my nurturing methods with love, respect, and admiration. I could do no wrong in their trusting eyes.

Each year, God placed in my class a student who struggled with a disability such as diabetes, asthma, hearing loss, or Tourette's syndrome. Some students reacted to their troubles by becoming withdrawn, depressed, or defiant. Most tried their hardest to appear "normal." And each year, God nudged, *You must convey to all of the students that they do not need to be created perfectly to be perfectly created.*

So, with each new set of students, I waited until the time was ripe and addressed the entire class, playing on the children's natural curiosity. "Someone in this classroom spent a lot of time in the hospital dealing with doctors and needles," I'd begin.

Instantly, I had the undivided attention of the class. Every child holds a morbid fascination with needles.

"This person, at the present time, cannot be cured and must deal with an illness every single day."

A few anxious students craned their necks, looking around the room as if expecting a deformed monster to lurk nearby. Others bit their lips, clearly uncomfortable.

"This person looks like you on the outside, but something doesn't work quite right on the inside. Even so, in the heart, where all of the things that really matter are stored, she is very much like each of you. She is here in this room with you. She has the same dreams, hopes, and plans as you. The one thing she doesn't have, but wants very much, is your understanding."

I'd pause for dramatic effect, every saucer-like eye in the room riveted on me. I sensed a collective holding of breath, waiting in bated suspense. The disabled child would squirm a little, thinking, of course, I was discussing him or her. I did this intentionally, knowing that when I revealed myself, an instant bond would be forged between the two of us.

"That person is . . . *me*."

After audible gasps, I'd whip out my medical paraphernalia and explain diabetes. I'd answer questions with honest candor, watching the way the classroom unwittingly extended compassion and understanding both to me and that significant child in their midst. Diabetes was the needle I used to prick protective shields.

I memorized reactions. The listless girl with hearing loss perked up, gawking in disbelief. The child in leg braces gave an impish grin, then set her mouth in a determined line. The diabetic boy brightened in excitement, then nearly burst with exuberant pride in our common ailment. I could feel their emotional connections like a warm blanket around me.

More importantly, I saw slow realization form in the eyes of my disabled angels. Those children with chronic illness saw that I was loved and valued in spite of my limitations. I was someone with special needs who didn't flinch at asking for help. I faced similar challenges and survived with joy. I experienced the discomfort of being different, but embraced my difference anyway. I knew their fears and questions, their confusion and anger. I was one of them. And since I was loved despite inadequacies, they opened their hearts to the notion that they were lovable, too.

I'd like to think that as the year progressed all of the students crossed a new hurdle—learning to love and accept themselves and others just as they were created. I prayed that the lesson of living with a chronic illness without fear made a lasting impression.

It made an impact on parents who noticed a difference in their child's attitudes.

"How did you get Alison to wear her hearing aides? She refused to wear them in kindergarten."

"Bobby's so excited that you are a diabetic just like him. Now he's actually trying to keep his blood sugar levels normal."

"Scott misbehaves everywhere but in your class. Why is that?"

Diabetes became the key to open doors of opportunity to share my faith without stepping on toes as a public school teacher. I sympathized with parental guilt, reassured them in their efforts at treatment, and explained how God had turned my disease into a blessing, how He used me because of my diabetes. Most of all, I silently thanked God for creating me exactly the way that He did.

He made me, a diabetic, a vessel of noble purpose.

The Lord will work out his plans for my life—
for your faithful love, O Lord, endures forever.
—Psalm 138:8 NLT

Blessed Father, thank You for Your faithfulness toward Your children! By Your divine wisdom, You lovingly designed and created me for Your glory! I know You work all things, even pain and brokenness, together for the good of those who love You. Reveal to me the unique and valuable purpose You have planned for my life. And I will rejoice in Your precious name with all of my heart! Amen.

PART 6

EXPERIENCE HIS LOVE

God Is Committed to My Well-Being

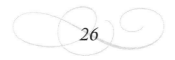

26

The Divine Pursuit

CECIL MURPHEY

There is nothing in all creation that will ever be able to separate us from the love of God which is ours through Christ Jesus our Lord.

—ROMANS 8:39 TEV

Throughout my life, God has pursued me—relentlessly. I don't mean that God chased me until I surrendered and became a Christian. In fact, the initial awareness of that unmitigating pursuit began five years *after* my conversion. It was also the first time I became angry at God.

My experience began during my second year of college, on a Monday, a day when I didn't have classes. I had sacrificed by not working full time so that I could study hard and serve God in ministry. On Tuesday, I faced a major final exam with two more finals later in the week; I had to spend the day preparing for those tests.

Shirley, my wife, woke up ill Monday morning and went back to bed. Our two preschool daughters weren't sick but were extremely fussy. As soon as I tried to focus on my studies, one or the other whimpered or commanded attention. If I stopped to take care of Wanda, Cecile demanded her share of time.

The mail arrived in the middle of the morning. Among the letters, I found our heating bill, for which we didn't have the money and wouldn't have it before it was due. We barely had enough groceries, and just enough gas in the car for me to drive to and from college the rest of the week. My car would soon need new brakes, and I had no idea how I could afford to have them replaced.

No matter what I did that morning to find study time, nothing improved. At least a dozen times I pleaded with God for help, adding, "I'm doing this so I can serve You better."

Despite my prayers, nothing changed at our house, other than that the girls fussed even more. By noon, I had not studied more than three or four minutes at any one time. A headache came upon me suddenly, and I'm one of those people who rarely suffers such an affliction. It felt as if someone had stretched a heavy band around the top of my head and continued to tighten it.

Despite their crankiness, I fed Wanda and Cecile their lunch and put them down for a nap. My head ached so badly that I gave in and laid down on the sofa.

As quietness filled our house, I felt anything but peaceful. As I lay there, I reviewed my situation. I had grown tired of scraping money together every month and never having anything left over. Saving for bad days ahead was a joke; we were *living* in the bad days. My good friends at church were serving God while pursuing lucrative careers.

The tension had been building for weeks. No matter how carefully we managed our finances, unexpected expenses sneaked in. I thought, *I'm in debt because I'm studying to serve a God who won't provide money to pay my bills.* For perhaps ten minutes, I grumbled about all of heaven's mistreatment. *Why am I serving God anyway? Others don't have these problems. None of my friends has to pray for money just to pay the bills.*

As my reasoning intensified, so did my anger. Then rage erupted: "I'm through with You, God!" I said aloud. "If You're all-powerful and all-loving, why don't You do something good for me? Why do you make it so hard to serve You?"

Instead of feeling better, the bitterness spewed out. "I don't believe in You any longer. What have I gotten from You except poverty and sacrifice? Besides, as a Christian, I always have to seek guidance. Before my conversion, I just decided what I wanted and did it. That's the way I want to live from now on."

The more I thought of the freedom from checking in with God and waiting for guidance that didn't always come, the more I liked the idea.

"I'm through with Christianity."

Almost immediately, peace flooded me. I was free from God. I had made the decision; now I could divorce myself from any connection with the church or Jesus Christ. I would take my final exam the next day and the other two I had later in the week. After that, I would drop out of college and get a full-time job, perhaps continuing my education part time. I didn't want to serve God; I was finished with all of that religious business. I had tried it, and it hadn't worked. It was time to enjoy my life and do what I wanted to do. I would never attend another church activity or read the Bible again.

But what about Wanda and Cecile?

That question burst from inside me. It was all right for me to choose not to follow God, but what about them?

"Shirley can take them to church if she wants to," I decided.

She's supposed to take over all of the spiritual guidance?

Yes, I decided, she could do it. She would have to do it because I was through with God. For five years I had sought God, and what good had it done me? I didn't want to think about God ever again. From now on, I would focus on what I wanted. If the Bible should turn out to be true and I ended up in eternal torment, I didn't care. I just wanted to be free now.

What about your daughters? Do you have the right to treat them this way?

Then I exploded. If Shirley and the girls hadn't been asleep upstairs, I would have screamed at God so loudly that neighbors would have heard my roar.

"That isn't fair!"

God had smacked me with a sharp left hook. I didn't care about myself, but I couldn't gamble on the salvation of my girls. My anger intensified, and I told God so.

Just then I remembered an ad I had seen years earlier in a Christian magazine; an organization that reached out to alcoholics wanted financial support. The picture showed a man trapped inside a whiskey bottle. The agonized expression on his face, along with his outstretched hands, showed that he couldn't extricate himself from the bottle.

Yes, I thought, *that's just like me. I'm trapped. Penned in. God won't let me go no matter what I want.*

"What kind of God are You? I don't love You. I don't believe in You. I just want You out of my life! Why won't You let me alone?"

I don't know how long the railing continued, but it was for several minutes at least. Finally, exhausted from all of my angry accusations, I stopped, too weary to fight any longer. "Okay, You've got me. I don't like it and I don't want You, but I can't turn away. Are you satisfied now?"

Of course, I heard no response.

"Even when I want to get away from You, You won't let me go, will You?"

As I listened to my own words, something clicked inside my head. Tears filled my eyes, and an overpowering sense of gratitude engulfed me. God would not let me go.

Even when I didn't want to follow, God still loved me and wanted me. I lay quietly, my eyes closed, and silently gave thanks for the unrelenting love that refused to let me run away.

As I continued to lie there, I heard a song, one that I was not aware of ever having heard. A baritone sang,

> O Jesus, I have promised to serve Thee to the end;
> Be Thou forever near me, my Master and my Friend.
> I shall not fear the battle if Thou art by my side,
> Nor wander from the pathway if Thou wilt be my Guide.[1]

Then the tears flooded, and I begged for forgiveness. God wanted me so much that I could never pry loose the divine arms that hugged me tightly.

The end of the story is that both girls awakened, alert and happy, and begged me, "Daddy, can we go outside and play?" I let them out into the front yard, where I could see them enjoying themselves. For the next three hours—an unbelievably long time for them—they never came into the house. My headache disappeared as quickly as it had come. Shirley awakened in the middle of the afternoon and felt well enough to take over the girls' care. I studied for three solid hours. The next day, I took the test and ended up with the highest grade in the class.

Finances still troubled us, but a few church friends, although unaware of our needs, gave us money. Opportunities to speak in churches opened up, and each time I left with a handshake and an envelope with a check enclosed. We also paid the fuel bill a week before it was due.

My reason for sharing this story is that this was when I began to face the *God who pursues*—and pursues and pursues.

Scripture provides hundreds of examples of the Holy breaking into human existence, chasing us, wooing us, reaching out toward us, embracing us, and changing us.

For many Christians, the awareness begins when the Holy bursts into our lives and disrupts us, and we don't joyously welcome that disruption. Initially we resist, even though we know that God wants only good for us.

Many times throughout the years I've cried out to God (in my rebellious moods) and asked why I was the object of such a divine quest. I've never heard a voice from heaven, but I have learned this much: I'm not unique. This "stalking" goes on in all of our lives because God has called each of us "according to his purpose. . . . For God knew his people in advance, and he chose them to become like his Son" (Rom. 8:28–29 NLT).

I remind myself that the One-Who-Loves-Me-and-Will-Not-Let-Me-Go has grabbed my hand and holds it firmly. When I try to pull away or to go out on my own, the divine fingers tighten their grip.

God won't let me go. Even though I haven't always rejoiced in that fact, sometimes even arguing and screaming, I'm thankful that God hasn't stopped the divine quest for me. I also know that as long as I live, God will relentlessly pursue me to complete sanctification.

This is true for each of us, and it means that if we pause and listen, we'll hear the divine whisper, the love call, the sweet promises, the tender voice that beckons us onward. It's the Unyielding Savior who accepts us as we are, yet never allows us to remain as we are.

This is too glorious, too wonderful to believe! I can *never* be lost to your Spirit! I can *never* get away from my God!

—Psalm 139:6–7 TLB

Holy God, I am truly grateful for Your unrelenting love that will never let me go! Who am I, Lord, that You should pursue me, reach out to me, embrace me, and change me? You reveal Yourself even when I am not seeking You. I rest in the assurance of knowing that the Lord my God will always be at my side, and He will never abandon me. Amen.

Body Revival

VICTORIA JOHNSON

You are forgiving and good, O Lord,
abounding in love to all who call to you.

—PSALM 86:5

I was born in the segregated parts of the Deep South, one of eleven children. My brothers, sisters, and I worked in the fields of rural Louisiana, picking whatever crops were in season, while my father traveled north for months at a time, earning a living as a farm worker. Representatives from farms in rural Washington State would visit our community and load pickup trucks with men, driving them throughout the country to what they promised was the land of opportunity. Once the harvest was complete, some of the men would pool their earnings and buy a used car to take them back home; the men who could not afford the trip home would stay on indefinitely. It was always a relief to see my father walking down the road, home safe again.

It was close quarters living in our small dirt-floor shanty. When Mama would yell, "Come on kids, we're having fish fry!" all twelve of us would huddle around a hole in the ground. We'd collect wood, build a fire, and deep-fry some fish one of my brothers had caught in the river. While we little kids thought these fish fries were fun, the older ones knew that it meant that we were out of grocery money for the week.

Despite our financial poverty, our parents loved us deeply, and whenever we had money, family meals were a time of comfort and joy. When the crops were good, we'd feast on ham, biscuits with butter, mashed potatoes and gravy, sweet-potato pie, and fried okra. We'd sit around the table for hours, talking and laughing. These special times felt like abundance to me, and I began to associate food with comfort.

When I was five, my parents relocated the family "up north" to Washington State permanently so that my father could find more work and we children would have a chance at a good education in nonsegregated schools. I'll never forget the first day. As I peered into the classroom window, I was so nervous I felt sick. Here I was, one of four black children in the entire school, staring into a sea of faces, with not one person looking like me. Not one! The teacher tried to reassure me. "It's okay, Victoria. We're all the same, no matter what color our skin is."

Yet I wasn't seeing color. I was seeing little legs—pair after pair of skinny little legs. And my legs didn't look like that! Mine were big and round, and they rubbed together when I walked. The teacher continued to try to coax me into the room. "They are just like you," she said. I wanted to scream, *They're not like me! I have thighs and they don't!* As I took my seat, which felt snug against my body, I realized for the first time in my life that I was different: I was big.

Despite every attempt to lose weight and be accepted by the other kids, I never outgrew my baby fat. By the time I reached high school, I was obsessed with food and dieting. As soon as I got up in the morning I'd think, *What's for breakfast?* The last bite of Mama's homemade biscuits and butter had me thinking about what she packed me for lunch.

By the time I went to college, one of my friends had taught me a handy technique for keeping weight off—throwing up. I spent a good portion of my college years hunched over a toilet and trying to hide my habit, out of shame. Yet despite throwing up, I still managed to gain the freshman fifteen—and then some. Instead of paying attention to the signals my body was sending me—low energy, depression, and headaches—I'd reach for a candy-bar pick-me-up or a jolt of soda with lots of caffeine.

You know the old saying, "If you want to look thinner, hang out with people bigger than you"? That's exactly what I did. To soothe my emotional needs, I hung out with women who looked like me, thought like me, and ate like me. Believe it or not, I was their fitness instructor at the time. Unfortunately, we didn't view exercise as a way to gain health—it was a justification to eat more. My girlfriends and I would get all dressed up in our workout clothes, barely break a sweat, and then hit a McDonald's drive-through. "Sure, I'll have fries with that! I worked out—I deserve it!"

One day while I was leading the class, I felt a little dizzy. Ten minutes into the workout I fainted. When I came to, I thought they were kidding when some of the class members actually asked me to get on my feet before their heart rates went down! It was then I realized that maybe these people were not my true friends. Maybe I was not as important to them as I had thought. The realization hurt me deeply as I had finally felt like I belonged with their group.

The blackout incident prompted me to go see a doctor. As I sat with clipboard and pen in hand, I began to lie about my health history with no regrets. (Actually, this was the typical "me" at the time. Part of my lifestyle was not facing the truth.)

"Has anyone in your family ever had diabetes?"

"No."

"Do you . . . ?"

"Nope, never. I eat fruit and vegetables and drink eight glasses of distilled water every day."

Then the magic question: "How much do you weigh?" Well, when exactly? In the morning? Before PMS? After PMS? Not wanting to face the truth, I scribbled 130.

Then the nurse came in to get my vital signs. Managing to keep a straight face as she read my fictitious questionnaire, she hit the weight question and blurted out, "130?!"

"Well, last time I checked it was 130."

"Please step on the scale."

"Shouldn't I take my shoes off? And my belt—it's metal; it must weigh a few pounds."

After stripping to the bare minimum, I stood on the scale, holding in my breath and pulling in my stomach, trying to be lighter.

She whizzed the metal bar way past 130 before she clicked to 150, 160, 170. When the rule clicked at 175, I jumped off the scale in horror. Was I really that fat?

I was still in a state of near shock when I met with the doctor. What he said to me did little to soothe me. "Young lady, if you do not change your eating habits and your lifestyle, you are on your way to developing type II diabetes." Holding a large syringe and getting right in my face, he continued, "You will have to take this needle and stick yourself with it every day. You will become a pharmaceutical drug addict if you don't make a major life change!"

His words hit me like a hammer. I thought about my aunt who had her leg amputated because of diabetes and my grandfather who had chronic heart disease. The doctor told me I was headed for these same complications if I didn't do something—and soon.

After I left his office, I sat in my car and sobbed like a baby while listening to a thunderstorm outside—yet the storm outside didn't begin to compare to the raging storm I felt on the inside. I realized that I had been given great opportunities in my life. My mother and father had sacrificed to provide me with an education and a life of equality. I was not living up to their standards, and I was not doing my life justice in this condition. Did I want to continue down the same path of self-destruction and "poor me" victimization, or did I want to take control of my health? Did I want to be 175 pounds and uncomfortable, or have a body that allowed me to move freely? Did I want to be out of breath and tired at the end of the day, or have the energy to do things with my family and friends? I had to make a decision.

At that moment, I asked God to forgive me for not honoring the gift He had given me—the gift of life. I asked Him to forgive me for not honoring my body, my health, and my talents. I asked Him please to show me how to get well. I promised Him I'd do whatever it took to do the right thing.

As I lifted my head, the rain suddenly stopped and a brilliant sun broke through the clouds. Although some skeptics might say that this occurrence was nothing more than a change in the weather pattern, I know in my heart that I was receiving divine intervention. I felt a tremendous peace within me that surpassed anything I'd ever known. I just knew that I would find a path and be able to lose the weight. *Thank you, God!*

I started my car and headed home. Only this time, I took a different route. I felt a burning desire for change. I didn't drive past all of the fast food restaurants that I used to think were my friends.

From that moment forward, I continued on my path to a "body revival" and developed the principles I wrote of later in a book. It didn't happen overnight, and it didn't happen without some pain. I had to let go of habits that were comfortable as well as some relationships that I finally realized were not healthful. Yet I never gave up. When I veered off course, my faith steered me back. I studied the Bible, and I prayed and meditated.

In my quest, I came to the same conclusion that millions of other believers have reached: I needed God to help me fix my life. God and God alone had all of the answers. As I allowed Him, He began to guide and direct every area of my life.

> I will exalt you, O LORD,
>> for you lifted me out of the depths. . . .
> O LORD my God, I called to you for help
>> and you healed me. . . .
> I will give you thanks forever.
>>> —Psalm 30:1–2, 12

Prayer

Merciful Father, abounding in love, how is it that You care for me? Your love, O Lord, reaches to the depths of my despair to restore every area of my life. How abundant is Your goodness and lovingkindness toward those who call to You for help. My soul is satisfied, as with the richest of foods. With singing lips my mouth will praise You all the days of my life! Amen.

Patchwork Woman

SHAE COOKE

Cast all your anxiety on him because he cares for you.

—1 PETER 5:7

My life is as crazy as the tattered quilt that hangs at the foot of my bed. I found the quilt quite by accident one day while on a reflective walk. Jewel-tone colors caught my eye beneath a rubbish heap laying on the curbside. Normally, I am not a scavenger, but I felt compelled to investigate. It was filthy and stained, and it stunk like old cabbage.

I stuffed it into my tote bag and brought it home.

"Honey, look what I found in the garbage!" I said to my husband. "A beautiful old quilt—I'm sure it's valuable." I held it up for him to see.

"You're kidding me, right?" he said, wrinkling his nose. "Surely you're not going to keep that . . . that . . . 'thing'?"

"This thing, as you call it, has potential, and yes, honey—it stays!" As I headed for the laundry room, he twirled his forefinger close to his temple and mouthed the word *crazy*.

I didn't care what he thought of me or my new treasure. I felt lured to it. It had a certain patina that seemed vaguely familiar.

I barely recognized my treasure when I removed it from the dryer. A vivid metamorphosis had taken place. Although it was still tattered, it was exquisite—very old, likely from the Victorian era. It had no pattern, and yet each rich burgundy and velvety green fabric remnant seemed placed with purpose, blanket-stitched together with gold thread. Vibrant colors stood out against a velveteen background. It was frayed and threadbare—several patches destroyed by moths, and there were stains. Despite its condition, it held together.

Over the course of the next few years, the quilt remained draped over the railing of my bed. I seldom appreciated my special treasure, because during that time, I suffered a long period of severe depression. Anxiety and panic attacks badgered me. A combination of childhood experiences, relationship problems, and burnout tangled my emotions, and my body, mind, and spirit buckled. The day I received the diagnosis from my doctor, I collapsed emotionally. Although I was not hospitalized, they kept a cautious watch over me. I felt weak and miserable, full of self-pity. Nothing mattered. Confidence, self-worth, and joy eluded me. Even my quick sense of humor wandered. I let go of everything that mattered, and I was just about to let go of God.

God, why me? I prayed one dreary day. I decided that this was going to be my last effort. If *He* didn't care about me anymore, what was the point in living? *Why won't You answer me?* I lamented. He seemed so quiet. I flung myself on the bed and wept. When the torrent subsided, I felt around for a cover to dry my eyes and found I had drawn up my crazy quilt. I draped it around my shoulders, and something strange happened. It felt as though Someone had His arms around me. I became increasingly warm, almost as though I had turned on an electric blanket. My breathing slowed, and my anxiety settled.

With my eyes closed, I stroked the soft, velvety fabric and traced the outline of the stitching, as if trying to memorize the pattern. I thought of times so long ago, such as the day the social worker took me from my mother. I was only seven and felt a huge sense of abandonment. But there was something different about these memories. Jesus was in them. There He was—comforting me at my mother's funeral, holding me when I was born, protecting me in a car accident, saving me when I almost drowned in the ocean! Finally, I understood. I opened my eyes and looked at the quilt—God's answer was all over it. My life, haphazardly pieced, resembled it! My past was just as brightly hued, ragged, blemished—but God's "patina" was all over it.

I held a tattered end close to my face and nuzzled it. *He loves me just as well ragged and torn as He did when I was whole,* I thought. I examined the scraps and old rags and in my heart knew that He could make me beautiful again, too.

I fingered the mended patches. *Could God repair me as someone so lovingly repaired this cherished treasure?*

The golden thread was the most exquisite and exciting revelation. I tugged a loose thread and it remained steadfast. *Could He take all of the random pieces of my life and give me peace?* A tear slipped because I knew in my heart that He could.

I called out to the Lord and asked Him to become my Golden Thread. I lay the scraps and tattered pieces at His feet and asked Him to mend my broken heart.

My family still does not see the loveliness of my old coverlet. But I do. I love every shred of it. It took a crazy quilt to remind me of what God did and was able to do with my life. The "Peacemaker" fastened all of the remnants and dried all of the tears.

Yes, my old quilt connects me to God in a way that only He and I understand. Just as I won't part with my crazy old quilt because of its condition, He won't part with me because of *my* condition. He sees the "beautiful" in me—stains and all.

> I will be glad and rejoice in your love,
>   for you saw my affliction
>   and knew the anguish of my soul.
> —Psalm 31:7

Heavenly Father, gather me into Your arms today, that I may rest in Your tender, loving care. Wrap me in the comfort of Your unfailing love and heal my wounded spirit. Into Your hands I surrender the tattered scraps of my soul. As You stitch and mend, may You create a work of beauty in me. Thank You, Father, for lifting my burdens and saturating my heart with Your unconditional love! Amen.

29

Taking the Plunge

BRYANT L. HEFLIN

The LORD is faithful to all his promises
and loving toward all he has made.

—PSALM 145:13

My pulse quickened as I crossed the gleaming marble floor of the spacious lobby and waited for the elevator. Ten years with the same Fortune 500 company and yet another corporate merger. Another reduction in force. The elevator door opened, and I stepped inside while ticking through a mental checklist. Crisp suit. Power tie. Polished shoes. On time.

For eighteen years, I enjoyed my career in the laboratory technology field and my current position as a medical sales representative. But now the travel, the hours, and the pressure were taking a toll on me both mentally and physically. All my time on the road away from home was taking a toll on my family.

I need direction, Lord! I prayed. Although I was well prepared for this crucial meeting, my heart sank into my gut as the elevator ascended to the fourteenth floor. A company-wide mandate required every employee to "reinterview" for his or her current position, forcing us to compete against employees of the "other" company for our own jobs.

My throat went dry as I walked down the hall to conference room B for an interview with the division's new corporate executive. My career and future were in his hands.

"Hello, Bill." I smiled and extended my hand. "Great to meet you. I'm Bryant Heflin."

The interview progressed smoothly, but in the back of my mind I wrestled with a rising dissatisfaction of my present occupation. Every time my company bought out another company, there were changes—changes for the worse. More products to learn. More territory to cover. More time on the road away from my wife and children. Despite all of the perks, the lucrative salary, and the opportunity for advancement, my sales career was losing its luster. The corporate world was no longer for me. For the first time in my life, I felt overwhelmed by the pressure and the pace. For the first time in my life, I dreaded going to work.

Bill "hired" me over my competition, assuring me of continued employment, but as the months passed, the downward spiral continued and I became more discouraged. Once again my territory was expanded. Once again my company asked me to consider a relocation, so I began seeking employment elsewhere. I had several great interviews for positions closer to home that required less travel, but the offers never came my way.

What is going on, God? Why am I having these problems? I questioned. *Do you still care about me?*

As the months went by, I plodded on. Gradually, God reminded me of "the call" He'd placed on my life when I was a college student, eighteen years earlier.

The time is—now, He spoke to my heart at last.

Lord, are You sure You're leading me into full-time ministry? I asked. With excitement and assurance, I sensed that this was His direction for my life. *If You want me in the ministry, I'm willing to follow Your plan.*

After a great amount of prayer and fasting, encouragement from my wife, and the counsel of Christian friends, I began preparing to leave my profession to attend seminary. Because of my extensive business travel, I had the opportunity to visit several seminaries. These visits clearly confirmed God's direction.

A seminary student with a family to support usually attends part time, but as I prayed and considered the stress that four to five years of working and studying part-time would place on my family, I felt led to pursue my education full time.

Fortunately, many institutions offered distance learning. All of the classroom activity takes place through books, tapes, and the Internet. This was right up my alley. I soon narrowed my school choices and made plans to quit my successful sales career. The money might have tempted some people to stay, especially after the year I'd just completed. But I had no doubt that God wanted me to leave my position and attend seminary full time.

This was exciting but scary. *How could we afford to live on savings alone while I attended full time? How could we afford to pay our bills, replace my company car, pay for tuition and books, and purchase interim health insurance?* It seemed impossible, but God assured me that He would take care of us.

Step out in faith, He urged.

It felt more like taking a plunge.

Once I finalized my decision, the Lord put an unexpected plan into motion.

After driving 45,000 miles per year for business and carting heavy equipment in and out of my van daily, I occasionally experienced a minor problem with my back. Routine physicals revealed nothing to be concerned about, but suddenly, my back pain flared up again. However, this time it was different. This time the pain was severe and radiated down my leg.

I scheduled an appointment with an orthopedic specialist. A physical exam and a series of X rays determined that I suffered from a congenital back disorder. My doctor ordered physical therapy and pain medications and immediately placed me on restrictions.

"No lifting more than 15 pounds. No driving more than one hour per day," he said. "Because this disorder is degenerative and irreversible, you will live under medical restrictions for the rest of your life."

Stunned by this revelation, I submitted the medical reports to my manager. The medical department quickly determined that I was physically unable to perform my regular occupation and placed me on medical leave. Although shocked by the sudden turn of events, I was relieved to discover that, thanks to medical disability insurance, I would continue to receive full medical benefits, use of my company car, and 60 percent of my salary for up to fifteen months.

A few days later, the admissions office of my chosen seminary called and I received a 40 percent grant on my tuition, the highest award given. In less than one week, God provided me with a car, health insurance, 60 percent of my usual income, and significantly reduced my seminary bill! As I stepped out in faith to follow His will, God generously supplied our needs.

After fourteen months of full-time study, I completed my seminary training and began seeking a full-time position in ministry. While on a brief camping trip at a local state park to spend time alone with God, study His Word, and seek His direction, the Lord placed a local Christian school system on my mind. I felt led to pursue a position as chaplain, ministering to students, teachers, and administrators. When I mentioned this to one of the principals, he was very excited.

"We've needed a chaplain for years, Bryant," my friend encouraged. "Please make an appointment to see the superintendent. And tell him I sent you." With his support, I pursued the leading that God had impressed upon me.

When I shared my vision with the superintendent, his face brightened with surprise and awe. "I've dreamed of initiating this type of position for twenty years!" After several meetings and much prayer, I became the first chaplain of this fine institution.

Everything was falling right into place. My new position began just before the medical disability benefits from my previous employer ended. However, I soon discovered that my new health insurance coverage would not begin until after a sixty-day wait period, leaving my family and me uninsured for thirty days.

What are we going to do now, Lord? I worried. With a wife, two kids, and a serious back disorder, having a lapse in coverage was a risk I could not afford. I looked into short-term coverage in case of a major illness, but the cost for just one month was enormous. I decided to call my company to verify the dates.

"Our records indicate September 30 as your last day of service," the Human Resources assistant stated. "However, I see that September 30 is on a Sunday. This makes your last *official* day Monday, October 1. Therefore, our insurance benefits will continue until October 31, the last day of the month of termination."

"Are you sure?" I asked.

"Oh yes, this is correct. I am sorry for the prior mistake."

"Thank You, Lord!" I shouted as I hung up the phone. Our old coverage continued until October 31 at midnight, and our new coverage began at exactly at 12:01 A.M. November 1. God provided for our need right down to the very minute. Isn't He awesome? God was in control of every detail in my life!

I thoroughly enjoyed the next two years as the school's chaplain. God blessed me tremendously with many experiences and challenges that prepared me for another opportunity He had coming my way. Another step of faith would be required. Another plunge.

As the end of my second year with the school approached, I accepted a short-term position at our church to work as a ministerial assistant during the summer break. Shortly thereafter, the school announced that because of decreased enrollment and financial concerns, many full-time positions were being eliminated––including mine.

When this news hit, I was relieved to have temporary employment already lined up. *Thank you, God, for providing once again!*

My search for a full-time ministry position was on again. As the weeks and months went by, it seemed that I'd spend the rest of my life waiting for God to open the right doors. However, as I prayed for direction, He began to reveal His plan. Over time, I felt Him calling me to become a church planter and pastor a new work. I wasn't sure I was capable. My family wasn't sure they were willing.

"What?" my lovely bride asked. "You want me to be a pastor's wife?"

We were hesitant, but God kept preparing our hearts. We gained valuable insight by meeting with a church planter and his wife. A few days later, I ran into an acquaintance, the local Director of Missions for the Southern Baptist Convention. He was unaware of my situation when he said, "We're looking to hire a few new church planters here."

My wife and I continued to pray.

After an interview with the local association of the SBC and an in-depth candidate evaluation, I was encouraged to pursue the opportunity. Then, after additional meetings and a season of fasting and prayer, my wife and I agreed that I should follow the Lord's calling into the pastoral ministry—and I became the pastor of New Life Church, an SBC church plant in Dayton, Ohio.

Looking back, I can clearly see God's providential hand upon my life. Once I stepped out in faith and said, "Lord whatever you want me to do, I will follow," He generously supplied all that my family and I needed and sustained us in His love during this lengthy career transition.

I believe that God waited until I took that step of faith to follow Him unconditionally before He poured out His blessings. It reminded me of when the children of Israel faced the Jordan River as they prepared to enter the Promised Land. Before them, the waters of the Jordan were at flood stage, running swift and deep. God had instructed them to "cross over," but nothing happened until the priests leading the procession plunged knee-deep into the rushing river. Then the waters parted and the Israelites walked across on dry ground.

I praise the Lord for providing me with the faith to trust Him and the courage to "take the plunge."

Let the LORD's people show him reverence, for those who honor him will have all they need . . . those who trust in the Lord will never lack any good thing.

—Psalm 34:9–10 NLT

Almighty Father, with everlasting love You care for Your children and provide for those who trust in You. I thank You for caring so deeply for me and being faithful in all that You have promised. With confidence and assurance, I follow You in every area of my life. Lord, You alone are worthy of all of my praise. I love You and will proclaim Your mighty name forever! Amen.

30

High School Heartache

NANCY C. ANDERSON

I will never leave you nor forsake you.

—HEBREWS 13:5 NKJV

I paced the floor and looked anxiously at the black-rimmed clock in the school cafeteria. I was waiting for my boyfriend, Jason.* He was supposed to meet me for lunch, but he was late, as usual.

I went looking for him, and as I walked around the corner, near the science lab, I saw him. He was walking, hand in hand, with my best friend, Jill!*

She had the decency to look away in shame, but he looked me in the eye, smiled a cruel smile, and casually said, "Hi, Nance." They just kept walking. I fell against the wall as my knees and heart folded.

At first, I was numb to the pain, but soon the anger of the double betrayal began to simmer and then boil.

I went through the rest of my classes with a steeled determination not to cry. I made it all of the way home. As I locked the door to my bedroom, I unlocked the door to my heart, and jagged tears bit my face. I cried until I was empty.

---

* Pseudonym.

Jason had been my whole world. He was one of the most popular boys at school and, when I was with him, I felt important. I liked being defined as "Jason's girlfriend," partly because I hadn't developed any other definition.

I thought, *How could he betray me so easily? And with Jill!* She had been a close friend since seventh grade, and I didn't understand how she could have done this to me.

I thought that my life was over. I felt like less than nothing.

I tried to pray, but I couldn't get my mouth to form any words. I picked up the Bible by my nightstand and held it to my chest as I simply said, "Help me, Lord."

I felt better. Stronger. I opened the book and read Hebrews 13:5: "For He Himself has said, 'I will never leave you or forsake you'" (NKJV). Then I thought of the song we often sang at church, "On Christ the solid rock I stand, all other ground is sinking sand."[1] I had been standing on Jason, and he had crumbled.

He broke my heart, but I knew that I would recover, with time.

In the next few months, I started to develop my own identity. I auditioned for a part in a play and was thrilled to get the part of Townswoman #3. I didn't have any lines, but I was happy just to be part of the team and to make new friends. I asked the Lord to help me be kind to Jill because she was the lead character in the play.

I started to discover things about myself—hidden treasures. I took a creative writing class and poured myself into it. I was the only one in the class to get an A+. I also volunteered to teach a children's Bible study, got involved in my church's youth group, and took a part-time job at a restaurant.

A few months later, I learned a valuable lesson as I watched Jason betray Jill and move on to his next victim. I never again measured my worth by another person's loyalty to me. As I learned to stand on the Lord and use the gifts He gave me, I saw that His love was consistent and unfailing. I knew that He would always be loyal to me and I would always be very valuable to Him.

I also learned that people will disappoint me and I will disappoint myself, but the Lord will never leave me or betray me.

I recently saw Jason at a class reunion and learned that he is struggling to hold his third marriage together. I married a wonderful man whom I met while I was attending Bible college, and we recently celebrated our twenty-fifth wedding anniversary. I can honestly say that I am thankful that my world crumbled while I was in high school because I rebuilt it on the Solid Rock.

Because your love is better than life,
my lips will glorify you.
I will praise you as long as I live,
and in your name I will lift up my hands.
—Psalm 63:3–4

Prayer

Lord Jesus, You alone are my Solid Rock! I will never be shaken. When no one else is true, Your unfailing love will uphold me. When it feels like I've lost it all and have no hope, You will be there beside me. For your great love endures forever! Although all may forsake me, You will never abandon the creation of Your hands. And I will always rejoice in Your everlasting love. Amen.

PART 7

EXPERIENCE HIS COMPASSION

God Is Overflowing with Compassion

31

A Cup of Forgiveness

EMILIE BARNES

To the Lord our God belong compassion and forgiveness.
—DANIEL 9:9 NASB

It was an unbelievably beautiful spring morning. A golden sun was climbing in a brilliant blue, cloudless sky, and the sunlight sparkled in the cool air. Bob and I had decided to have our breakfast out on the patio where our little fountain was dancing amid containers of pansies and mums.

Little curls of steam rose from our freshly buttered muffins as Bob read a page from a devotional for husbands and wives. We chatted about the grandchildren and the garden. Then, as we lingered over our fragrant cups of coffee, Bob pulled out our jar of *Mom's Canned Questions*. It's a decorated jar full of slips of paper, each containing a question designed to stimulate thought and discussion. We use it often when we have company and when we are by ourselves, and the questions have brought us both tears and laughter as they help us know each other better.

Bob passed the jar to me. I reached in and pulled out a slip. As I read, it seemed as though dark clouds were rolling in to block the sunshine. My impulse was to say, "Forget it!" and stuff it back in the jar.

What was on the paper?

Just this: "What would you do if you could spend one day with your dad?"

Such a simple question. But the memories it evoked had the power to fill my cup with pain, anger, and resentment.

You see, my dad was a brilliant man, a creative Viennese chef. He used to get standing ovations for the food he prepared. I'm told that he doted on me as a child, and I've inherited some of his creativity in the kitchen.

Yet my dad was also a raging alcoholic. Living in our home meant never knowing when he might explode. One wrong word and the spaghetti sauce was dumped down the toilet. The pots would be whipped off the stove and the plates off the table. There would be shouting and arguments. And although my father never physically abused me, he did take out his rage on my mother and brother.

In response to my father's rage, I almost gave up talking. If saying the wrong thing could trigger an explosion, I reasoned that it was better not to say anything at all. I became introverted and fearful, and many times I wished my father dead. When I was eleven, he did die, leaving guilt and resentment hanging over my life long after I thought I'd forgotten.

After my dad died, I still didn't talk much. When Bob and I began dating, he used to say, "Emilie, you've got to talk." And then wonderful things began to happen in my life. The most important was that Bob introduced me to Jesus, and I became a Christian. Then Bob asked me to marry him, and my Jewish mama (who was very wise) surprised me by giving her consent.

After Bob and I were married and I felt secure for the first time in my life, I began to talk. Now I even talk for a living—and there are probably times when Bob wishes I would stop talking!

Our lives went on. Our two children were born, and I threw my energies into making a home for us all. The kids grew up and left home. Through an amazing series of events, *More Hours in My Day* became a book, then an exciting ministry.[1]

I didn't think much about my dad. He was in my past, which I had put behind me. I was a Christian, and I knew that I was supposed to forgive others. So yes, I forgave my dad—or so I thought.

One day I went to a seminar that Lana Bateman was conducting at a nearby hotel. I didn't really know what it was about, only that my friend Florence Littauer thought it would be good for anyone. I walked into that room . . . and almost immediately my tears began to flow.

The Spirit of God had prepared my heart for a remarkable experience in coming to terms with my past and growing closer to Him. I realized that weekend that I still had a lot of pain concerning my father. I thought that I had forgiven him when in fact I had only boxed up my anger and resentment and stored it away—like sealing a bunch of toxic waste in a barrel and burying it underground. To forgive, I had to bring out that anger and resentment and hand them over to God, trusting Him to take them away from me.

That weekend, I began the process of truly forgiving my father and letting God restore my relationship with him. I admitted to myself that I needed healing. Although my dad was dead, I wrote him a letter, pouring out my love and fury, confessing the anger and bitterness I had held so long without knowing it was there.

This was hard work. It demanded all of my courage and energy. But what a difference that weekend made in my life! I poured out my cup of resentment. I let the Lord wash it bright and clean, and then I knew the wonder of having my cup filled to the brim with sparkling forgiveness—for my father and for myself. What a wonderful feeling!

But that was not the end of the story.

Not long afterward, someone mentioned my father. I was shocked to recognize a quick flash of anger. The resentment was still there, or it had come back.

What was going on? Was that difficult weekend in vain? Hadn't I emptied my cup of bitterness and let God fill it with forgiveness?

Oh, yes!

The forgiveness that I experienced that weekend was real. But now I was learning something very important about my cup of forgiveness: it leaks!

For most of us, forgiveness is an ongoing process, not a "done deal."

My cup of forgiveness seems to be one of the leakiest cups I own. It can be brimming over one day and empty the next—or refilled with bitter resentment over the same hurt I thought I had forgiven. All of this can be discouraging.

"God, I thought I had let go of that."

"God, I really want to forgive. Why is it so hard?"

But it can also be a source of faith, a reminder that we must keep going back to our forgiving Father for this cleansing elixir. We can't manufacture it ourselves; it always comes by the grace of God.

How beautiful our cup can be when we offer it to the Lord—washed and clean, as pure as the fresh-fallen snow, filled to the brim with sparkling forgiveness. All forgiveness—whether offered or received—is a gift of God.

Forgiveness, then, is an ongoing process of filling our leaky little cups, but it's not an endless cycle. Forgiveness has a forward motion, more like a couple gracefully waltzing across the room than a dog chasing its tail. Forgiving and being forgiven, we waltz forward along the paths of righteousness.

I know that forgiveness can happen. I know that the pain can heal. I know because of what happened with my attitude toward my dad.

Despite the dark cloud in my soul that darkened the breakfast sunshine that morning with Bob, I really was learning to fill my cup with forgiveness. When I read that difficult question from the jar, I felt pain, but I had an answer.

What would I do if I could spend a day with my dad?

First, I would take his hand, and we would walk and reminisce about when I was a little girl.

I'd tell him, "Oh, Daddy, I'm sorry for the terrible things that happened to you and made you the way you were. I know why you drank and were so full of fury. You had pain in your heart, in your cup—from being abandoned when your parents died, and from being a Jew in Nazi-occupied Austria, and fighting in the war and being shot three times."

If I could spend a day with my dad, I wouldn't deny the pain he caused me. It was real, and I've learned that denying real pain hinders forgiveness. I would tell my dad that I love him and thank him for the love he poured on me when he wasn't drinking.

And more than anything else, I would tell my dad that our heavenly Father can cover the hurt and pain and take it from us. I would want him to know my dearest friend, the Lord Jesus Christ, who said, "Forgive, and you will be forgiven" (Luke 6:37).

Of course, I can't spend another day with my dad, and that will always be a source of sadness for me. But I have finally come to a place in my life where memories of my father are no longer a source of bitterness for me. Forgiveness has cleansed the area of my heart where those memories reside.

True forgiveness—given or received—works because it changes me. And that, of course, changes everything.

You are a God of forgiveness, gracious and merciful.

—Nehemiah 9:17 NLT

I will joyfully sing of your forgiveness.

—Psalm 51:14 NLT

Prayer

Heavenly Father, thank You for the fountain of forgiveness that You freely offer to all who humbly ask. Cleanse away my anger, resentment, and bitterness. Fill me abundantly with your Spirit that I may offer a brimming cup of forgiveness to others. I praise You for Your eternal gift of forgiveness and redemption available to all through Your Son, Jesus Christ! Amen.

32

A Circle of Friends— A Circle of Hope

STEVEN CURTIS CHAPMAN

The LORD comforts his people
and will have compassion on his afflicted ones.

—ISAIAH 49:13

It was a typical small-group get-together for a typical small group— old friends and new in the early stages of trying to jell as a group. The things we shared were sincere but safe. Four couples and our kids— Mary Beth and I, Ray and Lori Mullican, Mike and Rhinda Smith, and Dan and Terri Coley—members of the same church and neighbors, all wanting to develop some consistent fellowship with a few friends.

On January 2, 1998, we gathered at the Coley's to watch the University of Tennessee play for the national championship. While we guys were enthralled with the game, our kids were rolling around on the floor, giggling, and having a great time. Our wives had varying levels of interest in the game but enjoyed the event, chatting with each other and keeping the snack foods coming.

At halftime, Mary Beth suggested that we go home because she wasn't feeling well. As we rounded up our three children, Ray and Lori were having the same discussion. "Ray, I think we'd better go, too. Alex and Erin need to get to bed before too long."

"Honey, I'd love to stay and watch the rest of the game, but I want us all to be together." Mary Beth remembers overhearing their conversation that ended with Ray almost reluctantly sending his family on home without him.

"Mom, can I stay with Daddy?" Erin, the Mullican's almost-nine-year-old daughter pleaded. They discussed it for a moment but then decided that Erin should go on with her mom and her sister.

About an hour after we got home, the call came. There had been a horrible wreck. While crossing a stop-lighted intersection, Lori, Alex, and Erin had been broadsided by a young man who ran the light. The only message we received was that things were serious. There was the possibility that the crash had been fatal.

I got in my car and made tracks for the hospital. My cellular phone rang. It was Mary Beth. "Steven, Erin didn't make it."

That short but tragic announcement literally left me speechless. I thought, *This can't be true. Surely, there's some mistake. Erin was rolling around on the floor at the Coley's with my kids just an hour ago.*

At times, we had some deep discussions about pretty weighty issues we were dealing with, mixed in with the usual small-group dialogue revolving around the typical hassles of life, but nothing like this—now we were confronting death together, one of our own, one of our kids.

How do newly bonding friends walk together in profound grief? What prepares us for funerals of little girls who die one week short of their ninth birthday? What do you say and not say to parents who have had their hearts ripped out by such a tragedy?

In the weeks following Erin's funeral, God began to work in ways that were new to me. It was as though her death was this huge boulder of providence that God hurled into the rather placid waters of our small group. The rippling effect, however, has continued to send out waves of grace, not waves of bitterness. It is hard to describe the miracle of God's love that we have shared together and the lessons we have been learning about true friendship.

One Sunday night a few months later, our small group met again. We had grown now with the addition of Al and Nita Andrews, a couple who had been friends with the Mullicans for several years, and Mike and Cady Wilson. That night, Al, who had become our "leader," began, "Tonight let's talk about hope. What does it really look like? What do you hope for? What does it mean to hope in the face of tragedy?" Al asked us. "A tragedy like Erin's death. . . . What are our options? We can either kill hope, abandon hope, or let it grow. How will we choose?"

As he spoke, I couldn't help but think about my experience a few months earlier of being a part of the combined funeral services for three high school girls who were shot and killed after a before-school prayer meeting at Heath High School in Paducah, Kentucky. This tragedy also hit close to home because of the fact that I had grown up in Paducah and had graduated from that same high school seventeen years earlier. Never in my life had I stared such grief in the face as at the funeral services of these three girls—and one month later, at the funeral for Erin.

How do people in the world deal with such senseless events without any basis for hope? It's hard enough for Christians. As our small group continued to meet, we became a circle of hope—friends committed to living out the reality of grace in the tension of the "already and the not yet" of our faith. As we have learned to grieve together as friends, so we have learned to rejoice together in the great truths of the gospel. In fact, it was from these experiences that I wrote the song "With Hope" for not only the Mullicans but also the families of Kacie Stegers, Nicole Hadley, and Jessica James.

Probably the culminating moment in this whole saga of Erin's death occurred as members of our small group gathered with others in a courtroom one year after the collision that took her life. It was time for the young man to face the judge and the consequences of his action. At the attorney's instructions, there had been no interaction between the Mullicans and this young man and his mom. Our church family had been reaching out to them, but this would be the first time Ray and Lori would see him. How would they respond? Like any good parents, the Mullicans had gone through seasons of great anger, confusion, hurt, and disbelief. But a year later, what would well up in their hearts?

The judge, obviously sympathetic to Ray and Lori's loss, asked them in front of all of us assembled in the court, "What do you want from me? What kind of punishment do you feel is appropriate in light of your great tragedy?" I could sense that he was willing to administer the full weight of the law if it would in any way help heal the crushed hearts of these parents.

Ray responded, "Your honor, we have prayed and decided to leave this in your hands and, more importantly, in God's hands. We only want what is best for this young man." I had a flashback to the moment when Mary Beth first spoke those words, which had left me speechless, "Erin didn't make it."

And now I was speechless again, left without words in the presence of such a manifestation of God's grace. I don't think I have ever witnessed a greater demonstration of the power of the gospel. After adjournment, Ray and Lori walked toward the front of the courtroom. I watched them give a sincere and generous embrace to the one who had taken so much from them. I overheard Ray say to him, "We've prayed a lot for you. How can we help?"

Friendship has taken on a whole new depth of meaning for those of us who walked together through "the valley of the shadow of death." Dan and I sat on his front porch one evening reflecting on the journey our small group had been through. We were both mad and sad. "I just want to be different because of this," he said. "How will this make us love our kids and each other differently?"

There is still much pain in Ray and Lori's hearts. How could there not be? But God has knit our hearts together in love. None of us is alone. There are still more tears to be shed and rejoicing to be shared between us, all because the gospel is true.

Praise be to the God and Father of our Lord Jesus Christ, the Father of compassion and the God of all comfort.

—2 Corinthians 1:3

Prayer

Father God of all compassion, You truly are an ever-present help in time of trouble and tragedy. In the midst of my heartache and pain, I will trust in You, for tenderly You embrace me when I weep. Securely, You carry me when I am grief-stricken. Gently, You comfort me with Your love. And by pouring out Your abundant grace, You give me strength to face the future. Amen.

33

The Real Healing

DORIS SCHUCHARD

"With everlasting love I will have compassion on you,"
says the LORD, your Redeemer.

—ISAIAH 54:8 NLT

Let's draw a picture of the autumn colors we saw on our walk," I suggested, rolling out the mural paper on the floor. I crouched down to join my class of kindergarteners, but my left knee suddenly refused to bend.

I must have overextended myself. These five-year-olds really keep me hopping, I thought as I rested that evening. *I just need to put my feet up and tomorrow I'll be sitting on the floor telling stories again.*

The throbbing pain did not go away though. A few days later, my other knee felt warm and tender. I was more tired than usual, and it became difficult to keep up with the energy of my students.

"You do have some fluid retention in your knees," my family physician noticed. "A few aspirin will reduce the swelling." But not even a dozen aspirin a day allowed my knees to bend more than 90 degrees; the pain felt as if I were opening a hinged door in the opposite direction.

Simple chores like trying to stand up after dusting a low shelf or picking up a book required more strength than I had, so I used a cane to limp around the house. Even so, it was hard to hold back the tears after a neighbor apologized, "I mistook you for a grandmother hobbling around your yard."

Over the next few months, other joints became infected. My jaw would lock so tightly that I could barely get a toothbrush in. My handwriting looked like a child's first attempts. Driving became tedious when I could no longer turn around to check the traffic behind me.

Most people would go running to the doctor, but I kept putting it off.

I'm only twenty-three, I argued, *too young to be detoured by illness. A little patience and the pain will disappear.* But the morning I was too stiff and sore to crawl out of bed, I was ready for an answer.

"You have a classic case of rheumatoid arthritis," the orthopedic surgeon diagnosed. I remembered my grandmother being helped out of a chair on the arms of my two uncles. The doctor explained that one in six people have arthritis. "We don't know the cause and there is no cure for arthritis yet, but we can control the pain and help you regain mobility." He was confident that he could help me, but I did not feel the same assurance.

I knew that my reasoning did not make sense, but driving home I worried. *My husband may as well enjoy his years with someone else. I'll be in a wheelchair by the time I'm thirty. I'd be too weak to care for any children we might have. And what if they inherit the same disease? Perhaps if I were older and had lived a full life I could accept this, God, but why now?*

I continued to teach and manage my home, but depression consumed my days.

I politely refused a friend's offer to play tennis and my sister's invitation to go shopping. Even a four-block walk to the grocery store now took a half hour. Certainly no one could understand what it's like to lose your health so young.

Fortunately, I did not have to feel sorry for myself for long. I began meeting others who encountered the same hardships.

A pastor shared his experience: "I've had arthritis since I was a teenager, but I don't let these knees slow me down in ministering to my congregation."

A college student, already on crutches, was also enthusiastic. "I can't wait to graduate and teach young children." These friends were not expecting illness to strike. Yet, they didn't let their physical difficulties stop them from leading full lives.

Arthritis didn't have to slow me down, either. Over the years, I adjusted to each new stiffness, taking walks with my own two children instead of running, sitting on a chair instead of the floor as I taught my students.

But the day finally came when walking from the parking lot to the grocery store or standing to prepare a meal became too painful. Sitting on the edge of the bed in tears one night, my hip bones locked together so tightly that I could neither stand up nor lie down. My husband took one look and said, "I think it's time."

I didn't know if it was a blessing or not when my doctor commented, "You're not old enough to have a hip replacement." At forty-one, it was comforting to be called young; on the other hand, chances are that I would have to go through this surgery again someday. And it's a challenge to be positive about a hospital stay—the noise, needles, pain, and lack of sleep—definitely not my type of vacation! My biggest fear was the anesthesia. *What if I never wake up?* After many nights of tossing and turning, I realized that I could fall asleep in God's arms and He would take care of the rest.

So I went ahead with plans to regain my mobility, thankful for caring doctors and the medical advances in this area of surgery. My doctor was pleased with the success of my operation. "You're moving well and ready to go home. Just remember, don't cross your legs, bend too far at the waist, or walk on your left foot for six weeks and you'll be ready to face the world again."

Over the next several weeks, I saw each of my needs provided for. A neighbor took over carpooling, Bible study friends cooked meals, my husband shopped, the children cleaned ("Thanks for the extra allowance, Mom!"), relatives and pastors visited.

Then why do I feel so sad? I thought that a dramatic crisis makes people more optimistic and appreciative of those around them. But I still had the same fears and "glass-half-empty" attitude toward life. Phone calls with friends, my family's weekend visit, hearing about my husband and children's day—nothing piqued my interest. I could focus on only the "can'ts"—I can't carry a laundry basket, pick a cup up off the floor, or put on my own socks. And so, with my squeaky walker to guide me, I hobbled off to the bedroom and cried. "I'm not satisfied, God; now I wish the anesthesia had lasted a little longer. I could join Rip van Winkle and sleep the next few months away."

I would have gone on this way if not for an unexpected wake-up call. One evening my mother phoned. "Your sister is being tested for cervical cancer." My younger sister, caring for an infant son after her husband walked out on her, could now be dealing with a life-threatening disease. I stopped crying for myself and with each prayer sent heavenward for her, I felt my own depression lift. Not only the physical pain but also my emotions and spirit were beginning to heal.

Through the Bible's encouragement, the support of friends, the doctors' expertise, and the peace for surgery—in so many ways—God showed me His compassion. I was never promised a life absent of hurt. Even with a new hip, I may never answer yes to my son's question, "Can you play football with me now?" But a healing operation has been performed on my heart. I can now put my arms around others, comforting them with the same comfort I've received from God (2 Cor. 1:4). That's the real healing. And one day I'll have that new and perfect body. I'm sure that you'll recognize me immediately; I'll be the one running and leaping across the clouds!

> The Lord is gracious and righteous;
>   our God is full of compassion. . . .
>   When I was in great need, he saved me.
> Be at rest once more, O my soul,
>   for the Lord has been good to you.
> —Psalm 116:5–7

Compassionate Father, I worship You! Comfort me as only You can, and I will rest in Your loving care. With the power of Your healing touch, remove the pain and restore strength to my physical body. Thank You, Lord, for lifting the sorrows from my heart, that I may run with perseverance the race marked out for me and proclaim Your holy name! Amen.

34

Unborn Dreams and Second Chances

STEPHANIE HITTLE

The Father of compassion . . . comforts us in all our troubles,
so that we can comfort those in any trouble with the comfort
we ourselves have received from God.

—2 CORINTHIANS 1:3-4

As a child, I learned the lessons of frugality and fruitfulness in my grandmother's garden. Oh, the wonderful meals that came from that garden! Oh, the work it took to bring those meals to the table! I preferred eating from rather than working in the garden, as my reluctance in helping with harvesting attested.

There were, of course, perks to being my grandmother's companion-in-work in the garden. Like tossing a vine-ripe berry inside your mouth.

I'd approach a red, ripe strawberry, gleaming in the sun with the promise of sweet fulfillment. Sometimes, however, my grandmother would say, "Wait," then point out the strawberry's decayed underside. I'd then pass it by for our gathering basket, but Grandma would intervene again. "Pick it. We can cut out the bad spot. I can use what's left in preserves," she'd say. Nothing was wasted.

God, like my grandmother, wastes nothing.

But that is something I couldn't see twenty-three years ago when, following an ultrasound during my second pregnancy, the radiologist pronounced my baby dead.

Dead. Before he ever really lived. It seemed so wasteful . . . all the planning and all the prayers. This much-loved baby was dead before we ever got to hold him, before he ever got to play with his sister, before his birth could bring us closer to completing our family and our dreams.

"Dead." It was as if I had been made of glass and now was shattered into little tiny pieces.

There were so many unanswered questions. It had not been a "problem" pregnancy. There had not been any warning signs. My first pregnancy had no complications. What had gone wrong? My doctors could offer no explanation.

"These things happen," my doctor said. "Try again in a couple of months."

My third pregnancy progressed as the other two, three months with no signs of a problem. When the doctor couldn't get a heartbeat for the baby during a routine examination, he sent me home to wait to miscarry.

I was unprepared for the sudden and violent miscarriage that followed. I lost a unit of blood on the way to the emergency room. I was hospitalized following a procedure to remove the remains of the pregnancy.

"Wait six months and try again," said my doctor the next morning. "It was just too soon. You've had one child, you can have another."

I so wanted to have another. My daughter had brought more joy into our lives than I ever could have thought possible. Motherhood was my first career choice. I knew that God had asked us to "be fruitful and multiply," so I had no questions about being "in His will." I told myself to accept these losses and move on to what I hoped would be my next successful pregnancy. I memorized Jeremiah 29:11 from my *New American Standard Bible:* "'For I know the plans that I have for you,' declares the LORD, 'plans for welfare and not for calamity to give you a future and a hope.'"

But eight months later, my fourth pregnancy ended in a miscarriage.

"I want you to see a specialist," said my doctor, and he explained that repeated pregnancy loss is the same as being unable to conceive in the fertility world. I was sent to an infertility specialist who diagnosed me with a hormonal problem. He put me on medication before and during my fifth pregnancy. I rejoiced when we heard the baby's heartbeat at twelve weeks.

I sobbed when we didn't at fourteen weeks.

I sobbed a lot. I worried more. People thought I was in a perpetual state of grief. Actually, I was spiraling into clinical depression and anxiety. Sometime after my fourth miscarriage my part-time communications job had been dissolved, leaving me even more time to focus on resolving my infertility. My life, as I planned it now, was to center around childbearing and childrearing. I grieved the past—the babies lost—and was consumed with worry for the future—that I would never again hold a baby of my own in my arms; that my "Norman Rockwell" vision of siblings seated around the Thanksgiving table would never be realized; that there would never be a generation of cousins at big family gatherings.

Infertility is not the threat of not having a baby. It is the threat of not having a family or, at least, the family one has always imagined. My friends were having their second and third babies. They didn't know how to console me, although many of them tried. Some offered, "God has a reason for this," but that confused me more. What reason could God possibly have in allowing my unborn children to die? Some just asked, "Have they found out what is wrong with you yet?"

I continued seeing the specialist who had a new theory of "what was wrong with me." With a new medical regime and renewed hope, I conceived for the sixth time. My husband and I felt the financial strain of my not working plus the infertility costs not covered by insurance, but we kept telling ourselves that it would be "worth it" when the baby came.

The baby didn't come. I miscarried again.

I underwent more tests, which resulted in a new diagnosis and a new medical protocol but without a different result. My seventh pregnancy also ended in loss. And, two years later, so did my marriage.

I had so many questions for God. I prayed but heard no answers.

In the five preceding years, I had lost a job, a marriage, and six unborn children. During that time, I had also lost all four of my grandparents. Less visible, but just as real, were my losses of self-esteem, security, direction, and faith.

The road out of this valley was long and gradual. I began to heal emotionally and spiritually with the help of professional counseling. I prayed a new prayer—not for a particular outcome but for a manner of being. I asked God to help me not to be bitter. I had seen others who had experienced pain in life become bitter and withered by it. I knew that without God's help, I would, too. I also asked God to help me be fruitful. I knew that it wouldn't be the kind of fruitfulness I had previously longed for; it would have to take new forms.

Romans 8:28 says, "And we know that God causes all things to work together for good to those who love God, to those who are called according to His purpose" (NASB). Causing and redeeming are two different things. God does not cause bad things to happen to people, but He can cause good things to come from our pain if we allow Him to. God wastes nothing.

At age thirty-seven, five years after my last pregnancy loss, I entered graduate school to become a licensed professional clinical counselor. A new career in counseling seemed a good place to use my communication skills. Previously, I had used words to inform or sell; through counseling I would use them to heal. By this time, my daughter was nine years old, and I had remarried. Juggling a child, a new marriage, and thousands of pages of reading and writing about psychology was not easy, but with God's help, I did it. From both professional and personal experiences, I learned how to help people who were hurting.

In the past decade, I have counseled hundreds of people who had loss issues. They come in anxious and depressed. Their plans and dreams—through lost jobs, lost relationships, or other circumstances—leave them in emotional places they never thought they would be. They need to regain a sense of themselves, find a new direction, and sometimes hang onto their faith in the midst of unspeakable and incomprehensible pain.

A student once asked me in the middle of a grief-and-loss workshop I was teaching, "How can you believe in God when such terrible things happen?"

"My faith doesn't give me all of the answers," I replied, "but it helps me live with the questions."

At times, sadness still comes over me regarding the loss of my unborn children—such as the time when my daughter's college sent out a "Sibling Weekend" notice, or when she, after baby-sitting twins, said, "Now I know what I missed." But I am not bitter, and I am fruitful.

Besides counseling, teaching, and writing, I, like my grandmother, plant. I plant vegetables and flowers. Last fall, I planted seventy-six daffodils. I hope for the best but am not sure what to expect this spring. The weather here can be unpredictable. Planting, like praying, doesn't always result in the fulfillment of one's plans. Whatever the result, however, God can bring something good and useful from the experience.

Because of the Lord's great love we are not consumed,
for his compassions never fail.
They are new every morning;
great is your faithfulness.

—Lamentations 3:22–23

O Lord, You are the compassionate and gracious One who comforts us in all our sorrows. As a father has compassion on his children, so You have compassion on all who trust in Your name. Lord Jesus, enable me to trust You unconditionally in all of my grief, sorrow, and disappointment, knowing that You will redeem every circumstance for Your kingdom purpose. Amen.

35

Discovering Peace

DAVE DRAVECKY

*Peace I leave with you; my peace I give you. . . . Do not let
your hearts be troubled and do not be afraid.*

−JOHN 14:27

As strange as it may sound, I was at peace on June 18, 1991, when I
was wheeled into the operating room at Memorial Sloan-Kettering
Hospital for the biopsy and possible amputation of my pitching arm.
I even joked about it as I said good-bye to my family and waved the
arm, "Bye-bye, everybody."

My surgeon, on the other hand, had much less peace about taking
my arm. When I went into surgery, he was cautious, still hoping to
save it. Certain that it was time for the arm to go, I made that desire
known.

During the previous months, my arm had become more than a
nuisance to me. Sure, I had a limb hanging on the left side of my body,
but I could hardly use it. I couldn't grasp anything. I could still write
left-handed, but only after I used my right hand to lift my arm into
position and place a pen into my hand. Not only that, I'd been fighting a staph infection for more than eight months. Continuous courses

of antibiotics had failed to heal the open, draining holes in my flesh. My arm was leaking like a sieve. It hurt. Some days I felt better, then I'd feel worse. Physically, I was at peace with becoming an amputee.

I wasn't fooling myself by thinking, *This is going to be a breeze.* Not at all. I knew that when the arm was completely gone I'd have a whole new set of problems. But at the same time, I had a deep-rooted peace because I knew God was in control. I also knew He would give me the strength to get through whatever lay ahead. I was ready to move forward.

Even the process of the surgery affirmed that God was in control. The initial biopsy came back clean—no cancer! Based on that, it didn't seem to be necessary to take the arm. Yet upon further investigation, my surgeon, a professional with tremendous experience—one of the best in the world—was compelled to take the arm. It proved to be the right decision because the final biopsy confirmed that the cancer had, indeed, returned. I experienced a great sense of peace in realizing that God really did direct my surgeon's hand.

Following the amputation of my arm, I "got busy." Instead of focusing on my own loss, I spent five days walking from room to room in the cancer ward encouraging other patients. On the surface, I was serving others, but deep down inside were issues that I simply didn't want to face. It wasn't a conscious deception, but I later realized that when I was involved in other people's lives, it was easier to set aside my own struggles. Afraid to face how I really felt, I didn't fathom the reality of what I was missing.

Despite the fact that I was at peace with God and at peace with losing my arm, I was not as prepared as I thought for living as an amputee. Facing the physical challenges would be hard, but I knew that I could do it. But I had no idea of the impact that being an amputee would have on my identity now that I was no longer a "whole" person.

Battling cancer is hard enough, but for many survivors, myself included, cancer leaves us with an even tougher battle to fight—the battle with our identity.

In some respects, the amputation shattered the peace of who I was, as if someone had taken a beautiful piece of pottery and smashed it. I had to look in the mirror and face myself. It wasn't a pretty picture. I didn't like it.

If I've learned anything through my struggles, it's that ignoring the loss is a recipe for disaster. The recipe for going on with life successfully begins when we honestly recognize and grieve our losses. Only then are we ready to redefine and rebuild our identity.

When I lost my arm, I lost my career, my position, and my sense of identity. All I had ever done was play baseball. Who was I if not a pro-baseball player? It was a long, painful, and difficult journey to identify the real Dave Dravecky.

Nonetheless, I was a changed person. The questions of who I was, why I was here, and what I was supposed to do could not be held at bay. I was surprised to discover that so much of my identity was wrapped up in my arm and what it had been capable of doing. It had brought me joy. It had brought me money. It had brought me status. Nice homes. Nice cars. On the outside, I continued to adjust to my new "normal" life. But inside it was a different story. Until I came face to face with the personal losses that accompanied the physical loss of my arm, I was awash in a storm of denial, depression, and confusion.

As I struggled, God took me, like a broken pot, and started putting the pieces back together—redefining who I was in *His* eyes, not in my eyes or the eyes of others. God used the amputation as a way of forcing me to consider who I *truly* was. When forced to deal with my identity, I experienced a deeper peace than I'd ever known before.

That peace did not come without frustration. It did not come without pain. In fact, it came as a result of brokenness. It came through the refiner's fire.

When the heat is on, when we're feeling the pressure of suffering, we have to choose to seek God or fight Him. Like most people, I did some of both. I did my share of whining and complaining. I clawed and scratched my way through, but eventually I faced the "big question." It wasn't about whether I was a baseball player. It wasn't about what people thought of me. It wasn't even about what lay ahead on my life's journey. The question was about God and me, about whether I would trust Him in the midst of the uncertainty of life.

I walked out of that experience saying, "Yes! God can be trusted. I can trust God for the strength to live life regardless of what it throws my way. Not only that, I can even trust Him for the ability to experience joy along the way!"

Discovering that I can truly trust God has given me a great sense of peace. It's not dependent on anything that happens in this life—not even on whether I survive. That peace rests in God and His promise that I will spend eternity in heaven with Him. The real peace in Dave Dravecky is the hope of heaven, a hope made possible by what Jesus endured for my sake on the cross.

Sometimes I'm still scared, angry, and frustrated by what I have to face. Just because I struggle doesn't mean the peace is gone. I can always choose to refocus my thoughts on the truth. When I remember that I can trust God no matter what, my sense of peace is restored.

The ongoing challenge for me as I continue on life's journey is to allow God's peace to be more a part of who I am as I face the challenges of life. My hope is for all to discover and experience His peace in the midst of life's challenges.

We have peace with God through our Lord Jesus Christ. . . . And we rejoice in the hope of the glory of God!

—Romans 5:1–2

Lord Jesus, with utter humility I thank you for the profound sacrifice You endured for my sake on the Cross. Your ultimate act of compassion enables me to experience the everlasting peace of knowing that heaven is my eternal home. How grateful I am that Your peace is strong enough to sustain me through all of the fear, loss, and uncertainty that I face in life. May all who suffer the anguish of a life-threatening illness find comfort in Your everlasting love and peace in Your gift of eternal life. Amen.

PART 8

EXPERIENCE HIS GRACIOUSNESS

God Gives Beyond Measure More Than We Deserve

36

Amazing Grace

CHONDA PIERCE

*How immense are the resources of his grace, and how great
his kindness to us in Christ Jesus.*

—EPHESIANS 2:7 NEB

I think I was about fourteen when I first heard the words *manic-depression*. It seemed to me that when my father took his medication or worked with a counselor to deal with his stress, he'd be okay. But then the church he was pastoring would experience a great growth spurt, or we'd take a family trip that rejuvenated him. Something euphoric would happen, and he'd think, *I'm feeling so good, I don't think I need to take this stuff anymore.* After a couple months, the medication would be completely out of his system. That's when the mood swings would kick in.

My father would become emotionally and verbally abusive to family members. But he was more abusive, I think, to himself. For example, he had a gun, and many nights he'd kiss us goodnight and tell us this was the night he was going to put himself out of his misery so we could all be happy.

I remember getting off a school bus and wondering what it was going to be like when I got home. Either Dad would be in a great mood and we'd all go fishing, or he'd be a basket case. And Mamma, bless her heart, would be in the kitchen trying to cook his favorite meal and do whatever she could do to pull him out of it.

If only we'd fully understood that it was a physical problem. But we fell into the trap of thinking that it was spiritual. Unfortunately, sometimes in the church there's a stigma attached to depression. We equate it with spiritual need, but sometimes it's nothing more than a physical need, the same as if your body needs insulin.

I'm not saying that God doesn't heal in response to our prayers. We prayed *a lot*. But the apostle Paul wrote that he'd become grateful for his thorn in the flesh because it was the very thing that kept him close to the Lord. And I've decided, oddly enough, that maybe this was our thorn in the flesh—something to keep our whole family clinging to Christ.

My mother played the role of the perfect wife, mother, and homemaker. She realized that since she couldn't fix the problem, she would just try to survive. Besides, she had made a vow "in sickness and in health." She worked overtime to ensure that our eyes remained on Jesus, not Dad, not nosy church ladies, not even on her—just Jesus.

One of the ways I coped with Dad's problems was by being the jester. I've always been something of a ham, even as a kid. I guess I felt that if I could only get Dad to laugh, or goof off, or get his mind off it, maybe *I* could fix him.

When my older sister Charlotta died in a head-on collision, I tried providing a little comic relief by boisterously objecting to God's will for our family. Soon after, my father abandoned the ministry, packed his suitcase, and left the family.

Not long after Mom, my younger sister Cheralyn, and I attempted to put our lives back together (my brother Michael had married and moved away), Cheralyn was diagnosed with leukemia and died a month later. In a matter of twenty-two months, our family of six was reduced to a family of two.

That's when my humor started becoming confused, muddled. I became the queen of sarcasm.

I remember standing across from Cheralyn's grave at the burial, looking at my mother, and saying, "We're dropping like flies!" That was my way of dealing with it. But Mother knew that I laughed the hardest when I hurt the most.

That first Christmas without Charlotta, we tried to figure out if we should hang up her stocking. We decided to hang it. I can't remember when we finally stopped.

The first Christmas that we didn't have Cheralyn, I remember walking into the living room of our one-bedroom apartment—it was just my mother and me—and seeing my stocking hanging there all by itself. *This is the pits,* I thought. *Things could not be any worse.*

But, of course, my mother said, "I think it's the prettiest stocking in the world!" That's my mother—determined to celebrate life, not concentrate on death. She reminded me that *I* was still alive.

There are no magical words for people in the throes of grief. I used to hear "time always heals" *a lot.* But my take on that saying is that it's baloney. Time *doesn't* heal all things; it's what God does during that time that brings the healing. Time might ease the pain—but the pain's still there. You've got to spend the time wisely.

But let's be realistic. I probably said, "Hey, God, what gives?" once or twice!

I have to admit, I've thought, *I have every excuse to give up on God.* But I do know that as imperfect as my family was, I grew up knowing about the Lord. Even in all of our storms and struggles and bad times, there was still that little foundation, that little piece of light. And you can't get away from it. I know; I tried.

However, I always knew that my mother was praying for me, and it would drive me nuts! When I attended a secular university, I was probably the farthest I've ever been from the Lord. I was the life of the party—trying to drown out what was going on in my heart.

I remember late one night after a party when I was riding down the road in my old beat-up Chevette with the broken radio, singing songs as I drove along. All I could think of were songs like "Amazing Grace." It made me so mad!

You see, you can't drown that stuff out. And that's one of the sweetest promises in God's Word.

When you become the life of the party to drown out what you need to face, then there's a problem. That's what I did for a long time. I even used my role impersonating Minnie Pearl at the Opryland theme park—four forty-five-minute shows a day—as a defense mechanism to keep me from feeling.

I remember standing backstage at the Grand Ole Opry one night, and Minnie Pearl was there. She told me this old story that one of the announcers of the Opry told her a long time ago: "You got to love the audience, and they'll love you back." Then she said, "I want to make this more personal. You'll never really know what laughter is all about until you make peace with God and love Him first."

Well, in my state of mind, I thought, *My mother told you to say that!* It sounded just like something she would say. I was at such a searching place in my life, but I finally realized *that* was what was wrong with me—I wasn't seeking to know God; I was trying hard to forget Him!

Not long after that, after the birth of my daughter, Chera Kay, I was at my day job working in a music publisher's office when I heard a song about God's love called "The Saving Kind." After I heard it, I went in the bathroom, literally sick to my stomach. Of course, as a comedian, I see the humor in these things. I thought, *This has got to really crack God up. I've been in the church all my life. I've heard altar calls all my life, and I rededicate my life to God in the john!* But my mother taught me that there's no time like the present to get your life right with Christ.

You know what I finally figured out? God didn't do any of those things *to* me. He's done a lot *for* me. He didn't look down from heaven and say, "Okay, I'm going to do this to her and that to her to mold her character." No.

But here's what happens. You get on a highway and drive a little too fast when it's rainy. And one of the laws of nature that God created long before He created you or me—inertia—says that if you go 60 miles per hour and hit a puddle, you might slide into the path of an oncoming car and get killed in the collision. God could reach down and stop it—and occasionally He does. But sometimes life just happens. When I quit blaming God for everything, as funny as it sounds, it let Him off the hook. And it let me off the hook of trying to find somebody to blame for everything.

Stuff happens. But what we do with that stuff is up to us. It's either going to destroy us, or we turn it around to help somebody coming up the road. God doesn't force us; the choice is ours.

One day I wrote out Proverbs 3:5–6, "Trust in the Lord with all your heart and lean not on your own understanding; in all your ways acknowledge him, and he will make your paths straight," on a large piece of paper. I cut out each phrase, and then rearranged them on my bathroom mirror, putting "In all your ways acknowledge him" first. Then I placed "lean not on your own understanding," followed by "trust in the Lord."

I know that's not how it's written, but the first thing I needed to do was focus on glorifying God. Then I chose not to lean on what I can't understand. I can't fathom why this happened to our family; I don't know why people die. I don't know why children starve in Africa. So I leaned not on my own understanding.

When I acknowledged Him and leaned not on what I couldn't understand, I started developing this trust.

Today, Christ is a vital part of our family life. David and I make God a Person at our table, not something we just haphazardly pray to. We pull Him into almost every conversation. We have family devotions before we eat. I allow Chera Kay and Zachary to hear and see me pray. I let them hear me apologize for things I've messed up on. We work at being real with our kids.

My husband teaches fourth grade Sunday school, and I love my women's group. There's a group of ladies who keep my performance schedule in the church office and pray for me. My pastor calls me several times a month. And I have an accountability group I meet with to keep me focused—people who ask me the tough questions like, "What did you read in the Bible this week?" I love every bit of that. I need somebody to remind me that I'll have nothing to give if I don't fill up every now and then.

I've made a commitment to this particular body of believers not because they're perfect and have it all together—but because it's a group of imperfect people learning about and loving the one true, perfect God.

I fit in nicely with a bunch of imperfection. Isn't God's grace amazing?

Our Lord poured out his abundant grace on me and gave me the faith and love which are ours in union with Christ Jesus.

—1 Timothy 1:14 TEV

Gracious Father, my heart overflows with gratitude for Your unlimited grace and unfailing love! With patience and goodness, You gently draw me back when I go astray. Like a healing balm, Your lovingkindness mends my broken heart. Thank You Lord for renewing my life. To You, I give all of the adoration, honor, and glory You so richly deserve! Amen.

37

A Fine Life

PACHECO U. PYLE

The LORD is gracious and full of compassion,
Slow to anger and great in mercy.

—PSALM 145:8 NKJV

Van is a tiny East Texas town just north of Interstate 20. Locals tend to make its name two syllables—Vay-un. Active oil wells pump even today—on the school ground, by the funeral home, behind the Baptist church, across the street from modest duplexes, and anywhere else the oil is still flowing in the quiet town. I live in nearby Lindale and visit friends in Van occasionally. Driving its streets, I remember what happened here years ago that changed my father's life—and almost prevented me from ever being born!

My father, Charles F. Umphress, was a young Dallas attorney, married to Sarah, a sweet girl from Lebanon, Tennessee. They were a handsome couple. He was tall and slender with brilliant blue eyes, a wicked smile, and a fine head of hair. She was a petite brunette with a pretty face and a sweet disposition. By early 1930, they had three daughters.

During the late 1920s speculators found a rich pool of oil in East Texas. Charlie and other Dallas lawyers flocked to remote towns to represent landowners in dealing with Big Oil Companies.

Charlie's Chevy made the trip to East Texas many times, sometimes loaded with other young lawyers. On a trip to Van in January 1930, they looked for some liquid refreshment at the end of a workday. Because of Prohibition, they had to settle for Jamaican Ginger, a medicine. In sufficient quantities, it would make them forget the pressures of their trade.

All of them drank it and waited to feel better; instead, they became violently ill. Charlie's colleagues lost the contents of their stomachs. Charlie didn't, and even bragged about his cast-iron digestion. A few weeks later, as he returned from seeing his East Texas clients, he had a flat. As he got out to change the tire, his legs buckled under him. Puzzled, he grabbed the car and tried to walk, feeling unsteady.

Remembering the Jamaican Ginger and the nausea, Charlie felt a deep dread. His buddies had emptied their stomachs. Charlie hadn't. He immediately recognized the symptoms of Jake Leg. During Prohibition, when liquor was processed without safeguards, some batches grew bacteria that produced paralysis in those who drank it and even killed many. Apparently, the Jamaican Ginger had harbored the same bacteria.

Drinking had always caused Charlie problems, especially when he used legal fees to buy liquor instead of make the house payment or buy groceries. But this problem was worse than just disappointing Sarah. This one was life threatening.

He finally got the tire changed and drove on, glad to be alone this trip. If this disease didn't kill him, it would certainly leave him paralyzed. Charlie was a proud man and cringed at the prospect of being a Jake Leg cripple.

He knew this road. A sharp curve with a large tree was not too far ahead. If he accelerated, he could smash into the tree, with no one the wiser. There was a life insurance policy, so Sarah and the children would be all right. He sped up, bumping over the rough spots in the road.

Suddenly he took his foot off the gas, stopped the car, and leaned his head on the steering wheel. He had used the premium money to buy liquor. In God's providence, the policy had lapsed, and Charlie just couldn't leave his family penniless. Returning to Dallas, he checked himself into a sanatorium, where he stayed until he had to leave for nonpayment.

Although he had the use of his hands, his leg muscles were shrunken. Charlie walked shakily on his tiptoes, unable to put his heels to the floor. Physically crippled and horribly depressed, he dragged himself to his office. He had already borrowed from anyone who would lend him money, and still he couldn't pay the office rent or the secretary's salary.

Well, he would quit practicing law, go home, and let the disease take his life. But God's providence intervened once again, this time in the person of an elderly bachelor from Madrid, Spain. Pedro Pacheco Martinez was a successful businessman in Dallas who owned a downtown tobacco shop and many other properties. Charlie handled the legal matters involving his rent houses. Mr. Martinez, a lonely man, frequently came by Charlie's office just to sit and chat.

Charlie cleared his throat and asked his client to sit down. "Mr. Martinez," he began, "you'll have to find someone else to handle your legal affairs."

"Oh! But why?"

"I'm a drunk, and now I've got Jake Leg. I'm not going to practice law anymore." Calmly and with old world charm, Mr. Martinez insisted that he needed Charlie's competent help. But Charlie said, "No, I owe so much money to so many people, I'll never get my head above water again." Mr. Martinez nodded, but asked Charlie please to withhold his decision for a while.

That afternoon, he sent his bookkeeper to Charlie's office with a check for a substantial amount, more than enough for Charlie to pay all of his debts. The bookkeeper also brought the files on twenty rental matters with the request that Charlie get busy and handle them because they had been neglected during his illness.

Years later, Charlie wrote, "No one will ever understand the profound effect his generosity and gracious manner had on me. It literally lifted me from the darkest gloom and despair to a pinnacle of confidence and hope. . . . Such an act can never be forgotten, and I was anxious to do something for Mr. Martinez that he in turn would appreciate."

He decided to name his next child Pedro. Since he and Sarah already had three girls, they were certain their next child would be a boy. I was born in 1935, another girl. Fortunately, Charlie didn't name me Pedro, but he decided to name me that second name, Pacheco. Mr. Martinez objected, saying that it would not be an appropriate name for a girl child.

"Why? What does Pacheco mean?" Charlie asked. "It's a surname, like Umphress," Mr. Martinez explained. "And it ends in an o, which makes it masculine."

"Oh, that doesn't matter!" Charlie said. He and Mother anglicized the pronunciation, calling me Puh-CHAY-kuh. So, the old Spanish bachelor had a child named for him, even if it was a girl and even if his name was mispronounced.

Despite Mr. Martinez's generous intervention, Charlie continued to drink until 1950. That summer, he determined to break the addiction and put his life back together. It wasn't easy. By that time, although he was only forty-seven, he had lost all of his teeth and couldn't afford dentures. He was unable to keep food in his stomach, and the skin hung from his bones. He described himself as looking like someone coming out of a concentration camp.

Once again, he had borrowed from everyone he knew. He had no more clients. The only thing left of his law practice were his books and a broken-down typewriter. Mr. Martinez was dead, and no other rescuer was on the horizon.

Yet Sarah stood firmly by Charlie's side. Determined to honor God in every part of their lives, they figured up the wages that he had earned and squandered in the past. Then they borrowed one-tenth of that amount from Sarah's brother and gave it to the church as payment of back tithes.

Gradually, Charlie's stomach problems cleared up and he put on weight. He was even able to buy some dentures. Attorney friends began to steer clients his way. He stayed sober and became active in the church he had attended as a child. Before long, Charlie was the teacher of the men's Bible class. Then he became active in The Gideons International and even served as state president for two terms. His legs remained crippled, but in every important way, he lived strong and free.

Before Charlie died at age ninety-one, he told my sisters and me about a conversation he had with God. "I asked God, 'Why did You bless someone like me? I'm a no-good. I wasted everything You gave me—my mind, my health, the love of my wife and children! Yet now You've prospered me and given me honor? Why?'" Tears in his eyes and his voice breaking, he continued, "God told me that in the eternal realms He can hold me up to all the hosts of heaven and to the Devil himself and say, 'Look at Charlie Umphress. See the first part of his life? See what a mess it was when he was in charge! But look at how fine I made it when he put Me in charge!'"

I'm glad I live near Van. Visiting there reminds me that God doesn't give up on us. And when He's in charge, He can make a fine life.

The Lord's kindness never fails! If he had not been merciful, we would have been destroyed. The Lord can always be trusted to show mercy each morning.

—Lamentations 3:22–23 CEV

Prayer

Father, thank You for Your unlimited patience and faithfulness toward Your needy child. Though I walk in the midst of trouble, Your infinite mercy and love preserve my life, uphold me when I stumble, and lift me up when I fall beneath the weight of my burdens. In humble reverence, I praise Your matchless name! Amen.

38

Leaving the Gr-r-r Out

GLENNA M. CLARK

Godliness accompanied with contentment . . .
is great and abundant gain.

—1 TIMOTHY 6:6 AMPLIFIED

It's a good thing I was driving alone. Who else but God would put up with my complaining and muttering?

All the way home from Edith's party, my feelings wavered between envy and then guilt for feeling envious. Jamming my hand down onto the car seat, I fussed aloud, "Lord, I know I shouldn't compare her home to ours. But the difference is as glaring as the oncoming head-lights. Her home, like those of many of our friend's homes, seems to me more like a palace than a home."

I ranted on, as if the Lord didn't know what I was thinking. So, I told Him in no uncertain terms. It's a wonder the windows didn't get all steamed up. "Yes, her home is a mansion. Our home, on the other hand, seems to leave something to be desired. Well, it's a nice enough house, I'll have to admit. After all, it's what You have graciously provided for us. And You know as well as I do, most of the time I do enjoy it."

Then I continued, "Okay, Lord, there are these other times, like after being exposed to such luxury as the home I just came from, that I find myself gazing with longing at 'the grass on the other side of town.' Oh, Father, why do You let me go on struggling to find Your loving care of us? Life seems so lopsided!"

Driving along it was easy, too easy, for me to visualize walking through Edith's lovely home. *Imagine! She probably doesn't even appreciate her fabulous kitchen. And everything matches. Everything! Right down to the potholders even! And how about that customized planter room-divider? I suppose she has plenty of help so she doesn't have to work her fingers to the bone to keep her 'estate' looking so nice. My, oh my, does it ever look nice! Well. No wonder. How could she miss, with all of her antique furnishings, customized window dressings, imported Persian carpeting, hardwood floors, and unique knickknacks? It's too much. It's just too much, that's all!*

By the time I arrived home, I felt drained. It didn't take a specialist to diagnose my problem. Such a childish tirade all but shouted, "God isn't fair to me!"

My husband was sound asleep. It was a good thing. If he'd been awake, I might have poured out my tangled-up feelings of self-pity on him the way I'd been pouring them on the Lord. *My husband doesn't need that,* I realized. Then a thought invaded my heart, *Come to think of it, the Lord doesn't need it, either.*

Padding softly around our quiet little home in my old slippers, I began to sense the Lord's tender hand of conviction—and a change in my attitude.

I confessed my sin of bitterness and jealousy and of my discontentment with His provision for us. My prayer of petition came easily. *Lord, You know this isn't the first time I've felt dissatisfied after being with friends who have more of this world's goods than we do. But You also know that I don't want to be defeated like this any more. Please show me how to overcome this sin. Show me the way to grow strong and remain victorious. Teach me to walk humbly and with gratitude for Your provision.*

Resting my head on my pillow, I meditated on all of the verses I could recall dealing with "things" and jealousy. Unbidden, a certain verse slipped into my heart: "Where your treasure is, there your heart will be also" (Matt. 6:21). The Lord gently impressed me with the long-forgotten principle of being grateful for what He chooses to withhold as well as for what He chooses to grant. Peaceful sleep enveloped me in His forgiveness and love.

The next morning, I awoke with a song of praise in my heart for God Himself, not just for what He gives. Before the day was half gone, He impressed me with the truth that when I'm choosing to be thankful I'm not grumbling. "Oh! Yes, Lord! That's it," I cried. "Gratitude is a matter of attitude, and it is the way of escape from the bondage of discontent!"

Rummaging through the desk drawers, I found an unused notebook. On the first page, I jotted down my heart's prayer. *Lord, I want to write a "thank You" note to You every day, expressing my gratitude for something You granted us. Something money can't buy. May the prevailing attitude of my life be one of gratefully, joyfully focusing on Your grace. Thank You for Your longsuffering toward Your needy child.*

One result of my repentance and resolve is that now, even some years later, I can still enjoy others' luxuries and return home contented. Then, too, the Lord has allowed me to write a daily "thank You" to Him, so every day is Thanksgiving Day in my heart.

If you struggle, as I did, with a lack of gratitude, try writing a "thank You" note to the Lord every day for something He has given you—something money can't buy.

> Gratitude is attitude with the "gr-r-r" left out.
> —Anonymous

> But thanks be to God! He gives us the victory through our Lord Jesus Christ.
> —1 Corinthians 15:57

Lord Jesus, humbly I bow in Your holy presence. With abundant gratitude, I pour out my heart to You. Thank You, Father, for the immeasurable patience You demonstrate toward Your children. The world may offer many enticing trinkets, but nothing compares to the priceless treasure of knowing You! My true contentment is found in You alone. Amen.

39

That Song in My Heart

JOANNE SCHULTE

If you forgive those who sin against you,
your heavenly Father will forgive you.

—MATTHEW 6:14 NLT

At the age of eighteen, the thought of "they lived happily ever after" had captured my imagination and clouded my reasoning, to say the least. And so, without asking God's blessing or my parent's approval, I decided to get married. After all, we were both professing Christians, and we were "in love." Certainly these must be the only qualities to consider when getting married—or so I thought.

During our courtship years, we liked to sit close in church, harmonizing on our favorite old hymn, "I'd Rather Have Jesus." It tells about preferring Jesus over anything this world has to offer, even silver or gold, or houses or lands. We thought that we meant what we were singing.

In our busy married life, we didn't realize that the words of the song were slipping from our hearts. I continued going to church, but with two children and a job, many other things replaced my time with the Lord. My husband, on the other hand, stopped attending church, preferring instead actually to strive for silver and gold, houses and lands.

Minutes after the birth of our third child, he viewed our newborn son through the hospital nursery window—a beautiful woman at his side.

Divorce proceedings began shortly thereafter.

I was angry, hurt, and, yes, even embarrassed to be getting a divorce. *I never imagined it would happen to us—other people maybe, but not us! Lord, why?* My constant prayer seemed to go unanswered.

In the days ahead, my tears flowed easily and often. But it was usually late at night when I cried into my pillow and sobbed my heart out to God. Nothing anyone said or did could make the terrible pain in my heart go away. Nothing.

When our son was six months old, the children and I moved to an apartment. As a single parent, raising my three young children became my greatest concern.

"Who is going to show my boys how to do 'guy things' like play sports and fix cars? Who will be a *dad* to them and my daughter? I certainly can't do it." Sitting on the sectional in my living room, I cried out to my pastor, expressing worries about their future—our future. After praying for me, he encouraged me to keep my eyes on the Lord and to trust Him for whatever lay ahead. His words were comforting— at least for the moment.

This time was a turning point not only in our lives but also in my relationship with the Lord. On my own now, two roads were before me—one with Him by my side and one without Him. I couldn't travel both roads at once. I had to choose one road or the other.

"Lord, I choose Your road."

God heard this brief prayer coming from the depths of my soul and began healing my heart.

That's when I remembered the Scripture that says, "Trust in the Lord with all your heart, and lean not on your own understanding; in all your ways acknowledge Him, and He shall direct your paths" (Prov. 3:5–6 NKJV). I committed my future to Him, and in the days ahead, He would be faithful to "direct my path."

Through Scripture, He showed me my need to forgive my former husband (Matt. 6:14–15). I realized that bitterness had become part of me and might hinder my relationship with the Lord. I certainly didn't want that.

But, God, there is much to forgive, and I don't want to forgive, for I have been hurt so deeply.

In obedience to the Lord, however, I forgave him, and, with time, God healed the hurt that remained. Once I forgave, the bitterness disappeared from my heart, and an old, familiar tune took its place.

The Lord saw more work to do in my heart. Next, He reminded me of my disobedience in marrying someone He had not chosen. I had made one of life's most important decisions without consulting Him; consequently, I had made the wrong decision. Realizing that was true, I asked for His forgiveness.

"Lord, I don't understand why it was so difficult to forgive someone who had hurt me, while You, my example, so easily forgave me for hurting You." Even as I prayed, the answer came. It was His grace.

As only a loving heavenly Father can do, He drew me into a closer relationship with Him. I began rising early to start my day with Him— to read His Word and pray and tell Him that I love Him. He showed me that although others are unfaithful, He never leaves me. And although I am weak—He is strong. He became my strength, my joy, my all. Financial problems, finding good childcare, and dealing with my children's injuries from a serious automobile accident were just some of the ongoing struggles that I had to handle. His guidance and strength made it possible.

One of the many ways God cared for me was by leading me to another company, where I received a substantial raise and held a better position. And at that new company, after five years of being alone, I met the husband He had prepared for me. He had not only given me a companion but also, in doing so, remembered my tears and concerns from long ago. At last there was someone to be a *real dad* to my children.

Sitting at the piano recently, I began to play songs from an old hymnal. Seeing a familiar song from so long ago, I reflected on those years as a single mother. How wonderfully the Lord carried me through them and what valuable lessons He taught me. Tears filled my eyes.

"Thank you for that journey. I praise You for Your great faithfulness to me in directing my path."

Today I know what the words of that song really mean. Now I can honestly say, "I'd rather have Jesus than anything."

I will praise the LORD God with a song and a thankful heart.

—Psalm 69:30 CEV

Lord Jesus, I trust in You with all of my heart. Thank you for teaching me to obey You and follow You. Thank you for forgiving me and enabling me to forgive others. Draw me closer to You as I move forward on my journey. I praise You for Your faithfulness and graciousness. May my life show others how You give beyond measure. Amen.

40

Losing Control

CINDY L. HEFLIN

[Jesus said], "The thief comes only to steal and kill,
and destroy; I came that they may have life,
and have it abundantly."

–JOHN 10:10 NASB

The afternoon heat was rising as I sat impatiently in my new Buick sedan, stuck in rush-hour traffic. With two fussy and hungry little ones in the back seat, I was anxious to get home and start supper. Once again, we'd been out all day, shackled by my usual rush-about-town routine. I gripped the steering wheel, my head feeling the tension and my soul longing for the peace of God's presence.

I'd been a Christian for years, but lately life had been like a runaway freight train, speeding out of control.

While striving to be the perfect wife and mother, I kept busy trying to "do it all." While striving to please God, I kept my calendar full of church activities and other worthy commitments. My mounting health problems and my husband's extensive business travel kept me physically and emotionally drained. The strain of enduring a marriage on the verge of collapse kept me running. Running from pain—running on empty.

I tried to trust God with my burdens, but spiritually I was still taking baby steps. My struggles and shortcomings continually clouded my perception of God. I prayed and read the Bible when I could, but often I was too busy to really apply God's truth to my life.

As I turned into the driveway of our home, I felt frustrated and disillusioned. From the depths of my broken heart I cried out to God, "Is the abundant life You promise in Your Word real? Or is it just a myth? If this victorious life You promise is really possible, prove it!"

The next morning progressed peacefully.

"Ready to meet your new teacher?" I asked my firstborn as we left home at noon. I buckled her and her baby sister into their seats, backed the car down the drive, and headed for her kindergarten orientation at the nearby elementary school. One brief trip, then we'd return to play outside in the sunshine!

Or so I thought.

On schedule with time to spare, I sighed with a sense of satisfaction and pulled up to the stop sign at the end of our block. For once, everything in my world was at peace. Cautiously, I observed the street in both directions. Seeing no oncoming traffic, I pulled into the intersection and then—I saw it! A dull-gray Chevy barreling directly toward us!

Brakes slammed. Tires screeched. One metal-crushing instant later, the old paint-worn tank slammed into our left front fender and plowed the front end of our car aside like a pile of snow.

Horror struck me as wailing erupted. I checked the children and quickly pulled them from the wreckage. Miraculously, we escaped unharmed, mere inches sparing us from tragedy!

In the scorching summer sun, I sat on the sidewalk clutching my precious daughters. Shaken, speechless, and too stunned to cry, I stared at the crumpled debris. *How did we survive?* I wondered. *How did we escape unharmed?* Clearly, God had intervened.

"Okay, God. You have my full attention," I whispered. Tired of doing things my way, tired of running from the only One who could set me free, I surrendered total control of my broken life to Christ.

As the investigating police officer observed the dry pavement, the clear blue skies, and the twisted heap of metal in the intersection, he scribbled on a notepad and scratched his head.

"Was there *something* on your mind, ma'am?" He was searching for a plausible cause for the collision—and so was I.

All afternoon, I wrestled with the slow-motion scene replaying in my mind, and a knot tightening in my stomach. Fearful of the only probable explanation, I promptly scheduled an exam with the ophthalmologist.

Years earlier, I'd learned of a condition that would "someday" affect my peripheral vision and perhaps cause blindness. But soon after, I was "randomly selected" for a five-year research program that held the promise of a treatment, possibly a cure. *With God all things are possible,* I assured myself, believing that He was orchestrating a miracle.

Now that hope was gone. Nothing could have prepared me for the doctor's devastating report.

"Tests indicate severe retinal deterioration . . . loss of all peripheral vision . . . visual fields restricted to less than twenty degrees . . . never drive again."

Due to the severity of this "tunnel vision," I was now legally blind.

In the days and weeks that followed, those words haunted me and overshadowed my life, slamming the brakes on my independence. It crushed me to face my loss, my limitations, and the reality of the incurable disease slowly stealing my sight.

I had to learn to live with these limitations, but it was unpleasant. Reluctantly, I relinquished control as I began to depend on others for help. Reluctantly, I accepted in-home training from the Bureau for the Visually Impaired. Reluctantly, I complied with my rehab instructor as he coerced me to parade along the sidewalk of my neighborhood with a white-tipped cane, revealing my hidden infirmity for the whole world to see.

Lost in my despair one dreary autumn morning, I sipped a steaming cup of tea and scanned the overcast skies, searching for a glimpse of sunshine. While my children slept, I lingered alone deep in thought. Although I longed to feel the warmth of God's presence, my hot cup of tea did little to change the climate of my numb heart.

I whispered a simple prayer: "Lord, I need your help."

The children's playful chatter suddenly stifled my thoughts. Another day had begun. While I muddled through a typical morning of breakfast, laundry, and Play-Doh®, wrestled with anxiety, and struggled to understand, *Why did God allow this to happen?*

Somehow, I knew He would take care of our needs. But how? My husband traveled out of state frequently, for days, sometimes weeks, at a time. I was used to being on the go, shuttling our girls to preschool, play dates, and the pediatrician. I relished our spur-of-the-moment trips to visit out-of-town friends.

My independence was now stolen! The challenge of my visual limitations overwhelmed me. Unwilling to burden others, I felt uncomfortable asking for assistance. It seemed impossible to cope with these sudden changes, even with God's help.

The telephone rang as I collapsed on the couch, weary from a long afternoon and a heavy heart. To my surprise, the friendly caller was Mary, a young mom from our church. Despite our mutual friends, we'd never met. Compassionately, she expressed her concern for my family and me. "You know, I'm always out with my two children. I'd really love the company if you ever need a ride."

She offered to help me run errands one day each week.

A tear rolled down my cheek. I hung up the phone, feeling amazed and grateful. God had heard my feeble prayer, and faithfully He answered! A tiny seed of hope began to grow in my heart. After baths and bedtime stories, I kissed my girls good night and then fell into bed exhausted but with a new sense of peace. *Thank You, Lord Jesus, for meeting our need!*

Little did I know, God was providing my need for transportation and *so much more.*

Mary arrived promptly the next afternoon. Her bright smile and cheerful nature were as sunny as her buttercup-colored sedan. Each Tuesday, with the children buckled securely and with plenty of books and snacks, we set out for an afternoon on the road. Soon, I realized that traveling with Mary was more than just a trip to the bank, drugstore, or post office. It was *fun!* With games and songs, she entertained the children as we made our rounds *"all through the town."* Her joy and laughter were healing to my weary soul.

A "road trip" with Mary always included lively conversation that lifted my spirits. Discussion often centered on our faith in Christ as she encouraged me to seek Him for the strength to overcome every trial.

Mary had a joy for the Lord that I'd never seen or experienced. Something about her faith sparked my desire to draw closer to God. Being stripped of my wheels forced me to realign my priorities. I learned to put God first, study the Word, and surrender my pain to Him in prayer.

Before long, icy winds whistled through the barren branches that stretched across the winter sky. Housebound against my will, I felt shrouded in isolation like a tulip bulb trapped beneath the frozen ground. But a snowy afternoon spent at Mary's inviting home always cured my cabin fever. Over a cup of hot chocolate, we talked and laughed while our toddlers napped and the five-year-olds played Candyland on the floor nearby.

As I shared the strain these challenges were placing on my marriage, Mary listened patiently. "In seasons of joy or pain, always remember: God's love for you is greater than you can ever imagine," she encouraged. "We're all someone special in His eyes!"

The truth of her simple words shot straight into my heart, compelling me to keep trusting the Lord. My faith began to flourish as I pulled the weeds of despair and discouragement that were choking off its growth.

Soon the scent of apple blossoms in the breeze and the welcome sunshine of spring revealed a new hope in my heart. My despair subsided and my faith strengthened as I learned to focus on the Lord instead of my circumstances.

Adjusting to my loss of independence was difficult, but little by little, I learned that God was in control. "If it's God's will, God will provide a way," I often reminded myself whenever an appointment or a special activity was planned. And He has never left us stranded.

"Draw near to God and He will draw near to you" (James 4:8 NASB), I learned as I continued to study the Word. As I grew closer to the Lord, He began miraculously to heal my marriage and, eventually, my health.

Although I continue to live with ever-increasing visual limitations, I strive to focus *not* on what has been lost, but on what has been gained. Living with "tunnel vision" has enabled me to recognize an even greater challenge: my spiritual "tunnel vision." I've learned that "leaning on my own understanding" is unsound and potentially harmful. God alone sees the entire realm of my life, so I walk by faith, not by sight—for *His* vision is perfect. When I fix my gaze on Him, He will guide me safely through any circumstance.

During my darkest days, He "who is able to do immeasurably more than all we ask or imagine" (Eph. 3:20) provided for all of my needs and more. The shining light of the Lord's unfailing love transformed my heart and enabled me to see clearly—that I can overcome any weakness when I trust Him unconditionally.

Life truly *is* abundant when God is in control!

My soul will boast in the Lord;
    let the afflicted hear and rejoice.
Glorify the Lord with me;
    let us exalt his name together.
—Psalm 34:2–3

Heavenly Father, in humble adoration I bow down and worship You! Tenderly, You watch over me with everlasting love. Graciously, You answer my cry for help, lift me from the depths of despair, and saturate my heart with joy. Generously, You provide all of my needs and bless me with abundant life! O Lord, my God, with heartfelt gratitude, I will lift up my hands and proclaim Your glory forever! Amen.

You're Invited . . .

Experiencing the Great I Am was created to give honor and glory to our Savior, Jesus Christ. The testimonies presented within these pages illustrate how awesome and incredible God truly is, when believers place their faith and trust in Him.

Like our contributors, millions have discovered that walking with Jesus is the journey of a lifetime! But what about you?

Jesus invites you to journey with Him as well, to experience the abundant life found only in following Christ. He will be your faithful and constant companion. Though you may walk in the midst of trouble, hardship, or even tragedy, He will preserve your life and lead you through with His strength and peace, if you trust Him unconditionally.

A relationship with Jesus does make a difference.

To discover this difference found only through a relationship with Christ, He invites you to begin the journey of a lifetime with Him today. Simply follow these steps:

A. Acknowledge your need:

Recognize that despite your best efforts you are separated from a holy God due to your sin. God's Word says, "All have sinned and fall short of the glory of God." (Romans 3:23)

B. Believe in your heart:

Realize that God loves you and believe that Jesus Christ, His Son, died to pay the penalty for your sin. "God so loved the world that He gave His one and only Son, that whoever believes in Him shall not perish but have eternal life." (John 3:16)

C. Call on the name of Jesus:

Receive Jesus into your life by faith and trust Him as your Savior. "If you confess with your mouth, 'Jesus is Lord,' and believe in your heart that God raised him from the dead, you will be saved." (Romans 10:9)

Then simply pray something like this:

"Lord Jesus, I confess my sins and invite you into my life right now. Thank you for dying on the cross for me. I accept your forgiveness for my sins and trust you to be my Savior. From this moment on, I surrender my heart and life to You, Lord Jesus. Thank You for the gift of eternal life. Amen."

If you have just made the decision to place your faith and trust in Jesus, and wish to receive free information about the abundant Christian life, please contact the Web site below. We would love to pray for you as your journey with Christ begins, and encourage you to experience the Great I Am!

Proclaim His Glory! Ministries
www.proclaimhisglory.org
info@proclaimhisglory.org

"Be exalted, O God, above the heavens; let your glory be over all the earth." (Psalm 57: 11)

To read other inspiring testimonies, or to share one of your own, we welcome you to visit us at www.proclaimhisglory.org. Also, watch this site for updates about possible future collections, as well as guidelines for how to submit your story as a candidate for inclusion in one of those collections.

Contributors

We wish to express our heartfelt gratitude to each contributor included in this collection. Thank you for your willingness to share your powerful and moving personal stories. May these testimonies touch and transform multitudes for the glory of God!

Nancy C. Anderson (www.NCAwrites.com) is the author of *Avoiding the Greener Grass Syndrome: Growing Affair-Proof Hedges Around Your Marriage* (Kregel Publications, 2004). Nancy and her husband, Ron, often speak at couple's events.

Richard Anderson is the Pastor of Capistrano Community Church, a non-denominational church located in Southern California. He is married with two sons, both attending California State University Fullerton.

Emilie Barnes is the author of 60 books, including–*A Journey Through Cancer; Help Me Trust You, Lord;* and her popular Minute Meditations books. Emilie and her husband, Bob, are also the founders of More Hours in My Day time management seminars.

Norma Blackstock, an inspirational writer and speaker from Bessemer, Alabama, has four grown children, three grandchildren, and a husband of thirty-five years. She is the founder of WOW Ministries and living proof that God loves to take our woes and turn them into wows. Email: blackstocknr@aol.com.

Kim Cason resides in the Smoky Mountains with her husband and two children. They minister to thousands annually, who enjoy the warm hospitality and tranquil beauty of their elegant, award-winning country inn. (www.eightgables.com)

Steven Curtis Chapman, one of America's best-known contemporary Christian performing artists, is the recipient of four Grammy Awards and 47 Dove Awards. He and his wife, Mary Beth, are founders of Shaohannah's Hope, an adoption assistance and advocacy foundation.

Glenna M. Clarke and her husband, Burton, have been missionaries almost all of their 58 years of marriage. They have three children, seven grandchildren, five great-grandchildren, and live in Irvine, California.

Tim Combs lives in Ohio where he continues to teach and mentor students. He savors the time spent with his wife, Becky, and their two sons, Joshua and Jacob.

Shae Cooke is a single mother, and former foster child, whose "inspirational voice" is heard in print worldwide. Write her at P.O. Box 78006, Port Coquitlam, BC., Canada V3B 7H5, or shaesyc@telus.net.

Jim Cymbala has been the pastor of The Brooklyn Tabernacle since 1972. He is coauthor with Dean Merrill of the bestselling *Fresh Wind, Fresh Fire*. He lives in New York with his wife, Carol, who directs the award-winning Brooklyn Tabernacle choir.

Amy DeLoach lives in Manhattan, Kansas, with her husband of 22 years, Scott, and their five children. Twelve-year-old Zachary loves playing sports and recently received his black belt in Tae Kwon Do.

Joey Denton, currently youth pastor at Denver Baptist Church in North Carolina, is married and the father of two sons. A former collegiate golfer, he enjoys reaching youth with the message of Christ.

Dave Dravecky and his wife, Jan, have authored ten books and continue to share their testimony nationwide. In 1991, they founded The Outreach of Hope, a ministry that serves suffering people, especially those with cancer and amputation, by offering resources for encouragement, comfort, and hope through Jesus Christ. For more information, visit www.OutreachOfHope.org.

Sue Foster serves as a Ministering Elder at Capistrano Community Church. She and her husband, Steve, reside in Laguna Niguel, California. They are the parents of two grown daughters.

Linda Gilden is the author of numerous articles and books. Her newest book is *Love Notes in Lunchboxes*. Linda enjoys time with her family where she finds lots of inspiration for her writing.

Doris E. Hack volunteers as a "sustaining ligament" at Christian Adventures International World Headquarters in Daytona Beach, Fl. She enjoys tenth floor condo living, walking the beach, and visiting her 6 children.

Stephanie Hittle is a licensed professional clinical counselor (L.P.C.C.) in private practice in Centerville, Ohio. She writes from her home, an 1840s schoolhouse she shares with her husband, Andy.

Victoria Johnson is the creator of twenty-four workout videos, four of which have won Video of the Year awards. She trains professional fitness instructors and physical education teachers, and lectures on peak performance for the NBA and Boys and Girls Club affiliates. Victoria speaks worldwide to Fortune 500 companies, faith-based organizations, and churches.

Robert K. Lemaster and his wife, Vicki, are members of Southeast Christian Church in Louisville, Kentucky, and have been married for 13 years. Bob has practiced as a registered nurse for 18 years.

Marita Littauer is a professional speaker with over twenty-five years experience and the President of CLASServices Inc., an organization that provides resources, training, and promotion for speakers and authors (www.classervices.com). She is the author of 13 books including *Love Extravagantly,* which she wrote with her husband, Chuck Noon.

Beth Moore is a writer and teacher of best-selling books and Bible studies, whose public speaking engagements carry her all over the United States. A dedicated wife and mother of two, Beth lives in Houston, Texas, where she leads Living Proof Ministries.

Cec Murphey has authored or coauthored over 70 books. He has earned masters' degrees in theology and education, taught school, mentored other writers, and served as a missionary in Africa. He and his family live in Atlanta, Georgia.

Chuck Noon is a professional counselor licensed in two states. He holds an MA in marriage, family, and child counseling. He has worked with hundreds of families and couples in many varieties of settings. Chuck and his wife, Marita Littauer, have been married 21 years and live in Albuquerque, New Mexico.

Lois Pecce and her husband are enjoying their "second childhood" providing daycare for their granddaughter. Lois is active in the Dayton Christian Scribes writers' group, as well as nursing home and children's ministries.

Chonda Pierce is a best-selling comedienne with an audience of 1.5 million nationwide. She's worked with Billy Graham, wowed the Grand Ole Opry, written eight books, and has four gold-certified comedy videos. Chonda resides with her family in Tennessee.

Pacheco U. Pyle loves to read and to write. With three sons and nine grandchildren, she and her husband, Bill, look forward to celebrating their 50th wedding anniversary in 2005.

Jennifer Rothschild, speaker, author, and recording artist, captivates audiences with her storytelling and signature wit as she travels across the country challenging her listeners to walk by faith, not by sight. Jennifer is cofounder of WomensMinistry.NET and is the author of three books including *The Unseen Hand of God* (Multnomah, 2004).

Doris Schuchard lives in Atlanta with her husband and two teenagers. She enjoys crafts, bird-watching, gardening, and writing in the areas of the family and education.

Joanne Schulte serves on the Board of Director's for the Orange County (California)

Christian Writer's Fellowship. She and her husband have a blended family of seven children and fourteen grandchildren.

Lori Z. Scott lives in Indiana with her husband and two children. As a diabetic of over twenty years, she loves how God uses her illness to proclaim His glory.

Linda Evans Shepherd is an international speaker, radio host, and the founder of the Advanced Writers and Speakers Association (AWSA) and Right to the Heart of Women, a ministry dedicated to women of the church. Author of more than fifteen books, Linda and her husband, Paul, have two teenagers. Visit Linda at www.sheppro.com.

Michael W. Smith, a popular contemporary Christian artist, has garnered 5 platinum-certified and 13 gold-certified albums, 3 Grammy Awards, and 40 GMA Music Awards. Founder of Rocketown, a teen club ministry in Nashville, he and his wife, Debbie, have five children.

Lee Strobel, educated at Yale Law School, was an award-winning legal editor of the *Chicago Tribune*. He wrote the Gold Medallion-winning books, *A Case for Christ* and *A Case for Faith*, and is a former teaching pastor at two of America's largest churches.

Karen Strand lives in the Northwest with her husband, Paul, a mischievous dog, and a bossy cat. Her book, *Escape from the Fowler's Snare,* gives a full account of the story told in this article. Visit Karen at www.karenstrand.com.

Bonnie Tackett is a published author of numerous poems and articles. A Boston native, she loves to testify about the Lord. Bonnie believes, "You can see Him in any situation if you look!"

Holly Tapley is in the process of learning a foreign language and providing medical care in a rural location of a war-torn country where life is anything but stable. She still enjoys bicycling.

Tammy Trent is a Christian recording artist and an author. Look for her new release *Learning to Breathe Again,* from W Publishing (June 2004) available in Christian bookstores everywhere. You may visit Tammy at www.tammytrent.com.

Lisa Weeks lives with her husband, John, and their healthy eleven-year-old daughter, Katlin, in Louisville, Kentucky. Katlin likes to swim, play basketball, and shop. She loves Jesus and has a tender, compassionate heart.

Permissions

A thorough effort has been made to secure proper permission for every story in this volume. If an error has occurred, please accept our apologies and contact Kregel Publications, P.O. Box 2607, Grand Rapids, MI 49501-2607, so that future editions may be corrected. To reprint any story included in this work, permission must be obtained from the original source.

We extend our deepest appreciation to each publisher and author who graciously granted us permission to reprint the following stories:

"Amazing Grace" excerpted from the article *Funny Girl*. Reprinted from *Today's Christian Woman* magazine (November–December 1998), published by Christianity Today International, Carol Stream, Illinois. Used by permission.

"Body Revival" excerpts from *Body Revival* by Victoria Johnson. Copyright 2002 Victoria Johnson. Reprint permission by publisher Health Communications, Inc.

"Changing a Life" taken from *The Case For Faith*—hardcover by Lee P. Strobel. Copyright © 2000 by Lee Strobel. Used by permission of the Zondervan Corporation.

"Crossroad on the Curve" first appeared in *Experiencing God* Magazine (August 1995), Copyright © 1995 by Linda J. Gilden. All rights reserved. Used by permission.

"Discovering Peace" reprinted from *The Encourager* Magazine, a publication of Dave Dravecky's Outreach of Hope, Colorado Springs, Colorado, summer 2001 and fall 2002 issues. Used by permission.

"High School Heartache" was previously published as "Boyfriend Betrayal" in *Teens: Living the Ultimate Challenge . . . God's Way* (White Stone Books, Inc. 2003) Copyright © 2003 by Nancy C. Anderson. All rights reserved. Used by permission.

"Leaving the Gr-r-r Out" first appeared in *The Lookout* Magazine (November 1991) Copyright © 1991 by Glenna Clark. All rights reserved. Used by permission.

"Losing Control" adapted from "Ray of Sunshine." Copyright © 2000 by Cindy L. Heflin. *Teatime Stories for Women* (Honor Books, 2000). All rights reserved. Used by permission.

"Mom, I'm in Control!" first appeared in *Focus on the Family Online,* April 2002. Copyright © 2002 Karen Strand. All rights reserved. Used by permission of the author.

"Run to the Cross" was taken from an interview by Tammy Trent on *Life Today,* August 2002. (LIFE Outreach International, Fort Worth, Texas). All rights reserved. Used by permission of Tammy Trent.

"Tested by Fire" first published in *Today's Christian Woman* magazine. November–December 2002. Copyright © 2002 by Norma Blackstock. Used by permission.

"The Divine Pursuit" excerpted from *The God Who Pursues: Encountering a Relentless God* by Cecil Murphey (Bethany House Publishers, a division of Baker Book House Company). Copyright © 2002 Cecil Murphey. Used by permission.

"The Gift," copyright 2000 by Linda Evans Shepherd. *Teatime Stories for Women.* Copied with permission by Cook Communications Ministries. May not be further reproduced. All rights reserved.

"The Greatest Lesson" excerpted from *Lessons I Learned in the Dark,* © 2002 by Jennifer Rothschild. Used by permission of Multnomah Publishers, Inc.

"The Magazines," by Beth Moore, excerpted from *Feathers From My Nest* (Broadman and Holman Publishers, Copyright © 2001), p. 153–163. All rights reserved. Used by permission.

"The Piano" first appeared in *The Pentecostal Evangel* (December 3, 1978). Copyright © 1978 by Pacheco U. Pyle. All rights reserved. Used by permission.

"Turning Point" reprinted by permission of Thomas Nelson Publishers from the book *Friends Are Friends Forever.* Copyright © 1997 Michael W. Smith.

"Vessels" was previously published in ". . . And He Will Give You Rest" (July 2002 newsletter), Rest Ministries, Inc., PO Box 502928, San Diego, CA 92150, Copyright © 2002 by Lori Z. Scott. All rights reserved. Used by permission.

Endnotes

Introduction

    1. Jim Cymbala, *Fresh Faith* (Grand Rapids: Zondervan, 2000), 119.

Chapter 1: The Greatest Lesson

    1. "It Is Well with My Soul." Lyrics by Horatio G. Spafford. Public domain.

Chapter 2: A Personal Test

    1. Words and music by Carol Cymbala, "He's Been Faithful." Copyright © 1989 by Carol Joy Music\ASCAP (admin. ICG)\Word Music\ASCAP.

Chapter 6: The Magazines

    1. Beth Moore, "Overcoming Food-Related Strongholds," in *Praying God's Word: Breaking Free from Spiritual Strongholds* (Nashville: Broadman and Holman, 2000), 148–68.

    2. Beth Moore with Dale McCleskey, *Breaking Free: Making Liberty in Christ a Reality in Life* (Nashville: Broadman and Holman, 2000).

Chapter 8: It Only Takes a Spark

    1. "Pass It On." Written by Kurt Kaiser. Copyright © 1969 by Bud John Songs, Inc. International copyright secured. All rights reserved. Used by permission.

Chapter 10: Jar of Clay

    1. "I Will Go." Written by Steve Green and Douglas McKelvey. Copyright © 2002. Performed by Steve Green, "Woven in Time," Sparrow Records, 2002. Used by permission.

Chapter 11: Run to the Cross

1. "I Love You Lord," by Laurie Klein, Copyright © 1978, 1980 House of Mercy Music (Admin. By Maranatha Music). Used by permission.
2. "Run to the Cross." Words and music by John Mandeville and Todd Moore. Copyright © 1998 Dayspring Music, a division of Word Music (BMI)/Patch of Blue Music. Sung by Tammy Trent from her CD, *You Have My Heart,* www.tammytrent.com. All rights reserved. Used by permission.

Chapter 13: The Goal

1. "Redeemer," words and music by Nicole Coleman-Mullen. Copyright © 2000 Wordspring Music, Inc./Lil' Jas' Music (admin. by Wordspring Music, Inc.)/Sesac. All rights reserved. Used by permission.

Chapter 19: Changing a Life

1. "When Mercy Becomes Mandatory," *The Atlanta Journal-Constitution,* 16 August 1990.

Chapter 23: The Hearing

1. "Redeemer," words and music by Nicole Coleman-Mullen. Copyright © 2000 Wordspring Music, Inc./Lil' Jas' Music (admin. by Wordspring Music, Inc.)/Sesac. All rights reserved. Used by permission.

Chapter 26: The Divine Pursuit

1. John E. Bode, 1868, "O Jesus, I Have Promised," *The Hymnbook,* Presbyterian Church in the United States, 1965, 307. Public domain.

Chapter 30: High School Heartache

1. "The Solid Rock." Lyrics by Edward Mote. Public domain.

Chapter 31: A Cup of Forgiveness

1. Emilie Barnes, *More Hours in My Day* (Eugene, Ore.: Harvest House, 1982).